Misery, You Don't Get My Company

Finding the Courage to Be Happy Again

Valerie Silveira

MISERY, YOU DON'T GET MY COMPANY:

Finding the Courage to Be Happy Again

Published by: The Still Standing Group

ISBN 978-0-9861104-5-0

Cover Illustration by Kalen Arreola

Jamie,

You were my first love. Until you were born, I had never known the kind of love I have for you and Sean. I am eternally grateful God chose me to be your mom; through all of the ups and downs of life, it remains my honor.

Had there been some way I could have removed the burden of your addiction Beast, or taken it over for you, I would have done it in a heartbeat. Even under the weight of your Beast, I always knew who you really were. As Sean says, you lit up a room. Thank you for teaching me about forgiveness and acceptance. The world is a much better place because you were in it.

I will always remember your smile, your laugh, the way your hand felt in mine, and how my arms felt around you. Your unconditional love of others will continue to inspire me. Little things still make me smile, and laugh, recalling your sense of humor and quick wit. I love that you always called me, mommy.

I promise to live out the rest of my days doing my best to shine my light in this dark world. Your spirit lives on in me and in my work, and I will keep standing and giving hope to others so they can stand too.

While I miss you every day, I am thankful you are free, baby girl and the hole in my heart will always be a reminder of how much I love you. Until we meet again, fly with the angels, Jamie Lynn.

I love you forever and a day,
Mommy

(In response, I can still hear you say, "lubadoo," something we continued to say long after you were a year old.)

<u>Author's Disclaimer</u>

This publication is not intended as a substitute for the advice of a healthcare professional.

My personal stories are told to the best of my recollection. Individual conversations and events were combined or condensed to stay on point. Some of the names of the people in this book have been changed.

In prior books and prior to her death, I referred to my daughter Jamie, as "Jordan."

Credit has been given to the author of quotes to the best of my ability. Many quotes are attributed to multiple sources, revised, or repeated so many times, that the original source of the quote might not be known.

I tend to use metaphors in everyday speech and storytelling and have found they are incredibly relatable to this subject matter. Therefore, I have chosen to use a few of them in my written works.

I apologize in advance for my lack of perfect grammar, or if my writing style wouldn't earn me an "A" in English class. It's more important to me to connect with people who need help than to write perfectly.

Acknowledgements

First and foremost, God is the reason I am still standing. By his grace and mercy, I am living as a woman of courage. Left to my own devices, I am pretty certain, the last part of my life's story would be quite different. I am grateful he has never given up on me and keeps reminding me I am the daughter of a king.

Rich Silveira, my husband, and best friend. Thank you for being my biggest supporter and cheerleader. Your belief in me allows me to take chances, knowing no matter what, you will always be by my side. I love you forever.

Sean Maher, my son. I can only imagine what it would feel like to lose your only sibling, your first best friend; to become an only child in an instant. Your strength and courage inspire me, and I continue to be proud of the man you are. Thank you for helping me to look at the memory milestones of Jamie's life in a whole new way. I love you, probably more than you know.

Shawnie Cahuya, my niece. I am inspired by your resolve to find purpose while living with two huge holes in your heart. Together, we can make it through anything. Love you, girl.

Pamela Turner, I have learned so much watching you navigate life with generosity and selflessness. I love you and thank you for loving Jamie, and for demonstrating every day, what unconditional love and acceptance looks like.

Dawn Ward, you came into my life for reasons I could not foresee. Thank you for your constant belief in me and my mission, your friendship, counsel, support, prayers, sense of humor, and so much more. I will forever be grateful to you for standing with me through the most difficult period of my life. I love you, my friend.

My love and gratitude go to Kalen Arreola. Thank you for the beautiful cover design, and for providing words to many of my thoughts. Your expertise is appreciated, and your friendship treasured.

I am grateful to Rich Silveira, Dawn Ward, and Lynn Chiupka for reading and re-reading the chapters of this book, adding your wisdom and insight. Knowing you have my back lets me write with abandon.

Thank you to my family for loving and accepting me just the way I am, and cheering me on as I become more. I love you.

Last, but certainly not least – thank you to the members of the Still Standing Sisterhood. It is my honor to know you and to guide in your journey. We are in this together. Love you, sisters.

OUR JOURNEY

There will be another angel

Around the throne tonight

Your love lives on inside of me

And I will hold on tight

It's not my place to question

Only God knows why

I'm just jealous of the angels

Around the throne tonight

~ "Jealous of the Angels"
by Donna Taggart

About Beasts

Beasts come in all shapes and sizes. Some arrive as the result of an alcoholic or addict in the family, abuse, abandonment, an accident or illness, loss, perfectionism, or something else. Many are a combination of two or more. A Beast is a situation, person, attitude, or circumstance that has left you lost, defeated, frustrated, angry, hopeless, helpless or living in paralyzing fear. Our Beasts remind us of the past, keep us from living the present, and fearful of the future. Lots of things are Beasts, and most people are living with at least one.

Beasts are not from God. I don't like to give enough respect to Satan by using his name, so I call him The Big Beast. If there is a school of Beasts, he is surely the headmaster.

The Beast only has a few tricks up his sleeve, but they are all powerful. Some of his favorites are guilt, shame, low self-worth, chaos, heartbreak, and fear. He will do whatever it takes to keep us living in these various states, or in all of them. The longer he can keep us believing we are not supposed to live as women of courage, the less likely we will, and the more miserable we become.

When I decided to stand up and claim my rightful place on this earth, as the daughter of a king, I knew who I was up against, but I also knew who was standing with me.

The more I take a stand against the Beast, the more he appears to back down, the way most bullies do. He does still come at me hard on occasion, so maybe he hasn't backed down at all. Perhaps, I have just become courageous enough to believe he has.

Either way, the Beast will not win in my life. I refuse to stay down on the mat. I reject the notion I am not worthy of making a difference in this world. I cover my ears when he tries to convince me my best days are in the past. I ignore his attempts to send me into misery due to the loss of my beautiful daughter, Jamie, and her unsolved murder. I laugh when he suggests women are not courageous.

Standing up to my Beast might be the most difficult thing I have ever done, second only to living with him.

Home Invasion

I was prepared, or so I thought. My daughter, Jamie (previously referred to as "Jordan") was very lost in the belly of her addiction Beast, and I knew the statistics. She had ridden what I call the Roller Coaster From Hell for fifteen years, and it didn't appear she was getting off anytime soon.

Over the years, I tried everything I could think of to help, force, guilt-trip, or manipulate Jamie into changing her life. As it became clear I had zero control over Jamie or her Beast, I became very depressed. My thoughts were centered on what Jamie was doing or not doing, and I found it increasingly difficult to concentrate on anything else. My heart was shattered into a million pieces, and I had no idea how to start putting those pieces back together while Jamie was crashing.

I felt like a failure as a mom, and I had let God down. I believed my best days were behind me and this was my life-sentence. I would spend the rest of my days with a dark cloud hanging over my heart unless Jamie became clean.

At my lowest point, I told my husband, Rich,

"I don't want to be here anymore."

I no longer wanted to live the way I was living. I was tired of feeling the way I had been for so many years, and I wanted out.

Thankfully, I found a tiny bit of hope and shred of self-confidence and made a decision that saved my life. I decided to stand up and fight; to try to get a little bit better.

Over the next couple of years, I got a lot better and even became happy again. I felt peaceful most of the time and was making a difference in the world.

My Beast was pretty much under control at that point in time. When he would knock on the door of my life, I tried not to answer, but he is clever and sometimes arrives in disguise. On a few occasions, I have made the mistake of opening the door and allowing him to stick his foot in the doorway. Thankfully, I recognized him in just enough time to shove him out and slam the door shut before he gained control of my life again.

Monday morning, August 29th, 2016, I sent a text to my brother Darryl,

"Happiest of Birthdays, brother! I pray this year is your best so far. Love you."

The cheerful exchange we had was no indication of what our next communication would be later that morning.

My office window faces the street and is close to the front door, so I typically get there first when there is a knock. I was on my computer, very focused on something, so I didn't notice the white SUV parked in front of the house or the young woman who walked up the driveway and knocked on the front door.

Rich happened to be walking by and answered the door. I tuned in just long enough to hear Jamie's name before he stepped outside and shut the door. I looked out and saw the SUV, and my first thought was that it was a bill collector. It was a reasonable assumption based on how Jamie had lived her life for many years. Perhaps subconsciously I was hoping it was a bill collector.

After a minute or so, I got up, went to the window next to the door and peeked out. A blonde woman around Jamie's age, wearing a ponytail, stood holding a metal clipboard; the kind that flips open to hold papers. It was the type a bill collector might use.

Then I saw it - the badge on her hip.

I opened the door and stepped out, taking a quick glance at Rich and then at the face of the pretty blonde standing on my porch.

"Jamie's dead isn't she?" It wasn't a question.

"Can we go inside?" she asked.

"She's dead isn't she?" I said it again, this time more emphatically.

The pretty blonde nodded and asked once more if we could go inside. My legs collapsed and Rich caught me before I hit the ground.

"No! No! No!"

It was a repeat of twelve years and twelve days ago – the first time Jamie had been shot.

Time seemed to stand still. Even today, when I think of that moment, it is surreal. I will never forget the second I realized my daughter had been shot again, only this time she was never going to gain control over her Beast. I would never see her again. My hope for her recovery was gone.

The young officer from the coroner's office came into the house, and we sat down. She told us Jamie had been killed the night before, but there was an active investigation going on and she couldn't tell us the details. Jamie's fingerprints and tattoos were in the system, and a positive identification had been made so we would not need to identify Jamie's body if we would rather not.

I tried to stay seated, but couldn't. Pacing the floor, wringing my hands, just as I had the day in the garage twelve years before, I said repeatedly,

"No. No. No."

Over and over I said it as if my refusing to accept what she said would somehow make it untrue. Maybe if I said "no" enough times, the officer would disappear, and this whole thing would have been a very bad dream. No matter how many times I said it though, or how much I paced, she was still sitting there.

When the officer left, I did something very strange. I had been making a change to my website when she arrived, so I sat back down for a minute and finished the change, even before making a single phone call. Shock makes people act in strange ways.

My first call should have been to my son, Sean, but he was taking a securities exam that morning. He was to call me as soon as the test was over, so I waited for a couple of very long hours until he called. Sean is very smart, but this is a hard test, and it is not uncommon for people to fail and have to retake the arduous test. Unfortunately, Sean had not passed the exam, and he was very down when he called. I asked him when he would be home because I wanted to talk to him about something. I thought I was doing a good job of acting normal, but he could feel it.

"Mom, I know something is wrong; just tell me."

"Let's just talk when you get home." I was very calm.

"It's about Jamie, isn't it?" He insisted.

There was no way I wanted to tell Sean while he was driving that his sister, his only sibling, was dead, but he could sense something was wrong, and he wouldn't let it go.

On that day Sean became an only child. It was the worst day of his life and the hardest phone call I have ever made. It was the day the Beast didn't just knock on my door; he busted it down. It was a home invasion.

Sean flew in the next morning, and we met with the detectives for the first time. Sunday, August 28th, 2016, around 9:15 PM, in Indio, CA, Jamie was shot several times in the chest at close range. She was 5' tall and unarmed. They had yet to piece together the details and had a long way to go to build a case. Jamie was loved, and people in the neighborhood where she lived were grieving, but reliable witnesses would prove scarce.

As the reality of Jamie's death sank in, I would go through a cascade of emotions. At times I would stand very strong only to fall apart. On some days I could talk about Jamie without crying, and other days I couldn't stop crying. There were moments I felt as if I could barely breathe.

Over the next weeks and months, I would cry, apologize to Jamie, find peace, yell at God, sit in silence, feel as if I would be okay, and fall apart. Then it would start all over again.

Lightning Can Strike Twice

Based on how and where Jamie was raised, her chances of being shot were probably as remote as being struck by lightning. The odds of her being shot twice surely were astronomical.

Perhaps the lifestyle she chose, changed the odds, but it is still something very difficult to wrap my head around. Of all the worries and concerns parents have for their children, this is not typically one of them.

My daughter was shot twice – twelve years and twelve days apart. The first assault was on Monday, August 16, 2004. In both cases, I didn't hear about it until the next morning.

It was a sunny Tuesday morning in the Seattle area as I drove home from a breakfast meeting and pulled into the garage. It was around 9:00 AM, so I was surprised to see Rich's car in the garage; he should have been at work.

As I opened the door and stepped out of my car, Rich emerged from the house. The look on his face was the same look he would have twelve years later, the day I stepped out onto the porch, joining he and the officer from the coroner's office.

This time he said,

"Jamie's been shot. He finally shot her, Val."

My brain struggled to comprehend what my husband had said. Was it possible I had heard him correctly, and Jamie had been shot? Rich said *he* shot her, and I knew instantly who "he" was. It was her ex-boyfriend, the one we had been trying to get her to stop seeing for three years.

I shook my head. "No. No. No."

Rich put his arms around me, but I broke free and whimpered, "No. No. No."

He closed the driver side door of my car and gently steered me toward the passenger door of his car.

"Get in. We need to get to the hospital."

"Is she alive?" I cried.

I struggled to free my arm from his grip, hearing his words but not wanting to believe them. I would not get into the car, for fear, if I did, this was actually happening.

He told me, "Yes, but we need to go right now!"

"Is she alive?" I asked him this question repeatedly.

Each time, he reassured me she was alive, and each time he insisted we needed to get to the hospital.

Eventually, I allowed my husband to pour me into his car, sobbing and gasping for breath. As a step-father, I cannot imagine how all of this impacted Rich.

My heart was beating out of my chest as I raced to the Intensive Care Unit.

With the help of a breathing tube, Jamie's chest rose and fell, as oxygen pushed into her lungs. Intravenous lines protruded from her arms and hand. Her face appeared swollen to me, but she looked peaceful, perhaps more so than she had in some time. I kissed my daughter and held her hand, tears dripping from my face.

Shortly after I arrived, the surgeon joined us in the ICU.

"She suffered a GSW to the abdomen."

"She had a GS-what?" I asked.

"A gunshot wound to the abdomen."

"Wait, I thought she was shot in the rear end." This is what Rich had conveyed to me on the ride to the hospital.

"It was an abdominal gunshot wound that entered through her buttock. There's no exit wound."

"You mean the bullet is still inside her?"

"Yes."

"Why didn't you get the bullet out?" I asked.

He looked at me as if I had asked the question in a foreign language.

"You don't understand; gunshot wounds to the abdomen are fatal. We spent hours trying to stop the bleeding and repairing vessels and veins. We weren't trying to get the bullet out; we were trying to save her life."

The surgeon explained the bullet had entered from the back at an upward angle next to her tailbone. It traversed her abdomen causing massive internal bleeding. An incision was made from her breastbone all the way down to her pubic bone. My daughter had been filleted open like a fish.

"It's pretty miraculous the bullet didn't do more damage. She's lucky to be alive," the surgeon explained.

For most of those years after the first shooting, I would have moments of disbelief that *my* daughter was shot. I would learn all sorts of things about Jamie's life, the legal systems, guns, and many other things I never wanted to know.

The life Jamie embraced was so far from the one we had tried to create for her. She never could, or would, explain her fascination with the world she had entered, and the people who lived there. Jamie grew up surrounded by people of integrity, in a loving and supportive home. There was nothing about her choices that made any sense.

I have heard lightning never strikes twice in the same place. I'm no scientist, but I can tell you lightning struck my heart twice – in the exact same place.

It felt as if my life ended when Jamie's did. I hadn't been miserable for a while, but I found out it is just like riding a bike. It is easy to fall right back into the misery trap. The day she died, I felt the pull of the misery magnet.

I was tempted to allow my grief to swallow me up, but I had lived in misery before and didn't want to go back there. I was at a crossroads with a powerful decision before me. I could stay down on the mat with my Beast on top of me, or I could stand up. Once again, I made the decision to stand up and fight for my life.

Taking On My Beast

Jamie lived with an addiction Beast for more than half of her thirty-year life. While her life spun further out of control, mine spiraled into darkness. I tried desperately to save her from herself, from her addiction Beast. As the years passed and I became increasingly aware of my helplessness, I became more and more depressed. I was living in misery.

Although I hid it pretty well most of the time, a dark cloud had settled over my heart, seemingly there for good.

While other parents enjoyed their daughter's high school graduation, college graduation, career highlights, marriages, and grandchildren, my hope of experiencing any of those things dwindled. Simply hearing about a mother-daughter lunch, or a family vacation sunk me further into depression.

I couldn't understand why Jamie would choose drugs, danger, illegal activity, poverty, and all that came with addiction, over her family and a "normal" life. I was frustrated and mad she wouldn't try very hard or for very long to battle her addiction Beast. I knew she was living with a powerful one, but I was discouraged because I believed with every fiber of my being that she could beat her Beast if she would just make the decision.

If only she could prevail, then *my* life could go back to normal. If she would just get clean, then life would make sense again.

Many years into Jamie's addiction, when I expressed to Rich how I didn't want to be here anymore, I realized I had hit rock bottom. It scared me to hear those words coming out of my mouth. Depression was not normal for a naturally happy person like me, but the longer I allowed my Beast to control me, the bigger and more powerful it became, and the more depressed I was. I lived in paralyzing fear for thirteen years, and it was destroying me.

I had never thought about codependency, nor had I ever considered myself a person that would live with it. Enabling wasn't as much of a stretch since I am generous and giving by nature, and I am a mom. It was time to start thinking about these things and to recognize what I was dealing with – the Codependent Enabler Beast. I finally made a decision to take on the Beast and to stay in the fight as long as it took, and no matter what I had to do.

So, there I was in the ring, staring in the face of my Beast, and I knew we were in for an epic battle. I stood up to him, and he knocked me down. I got back up, and he dropped me to the floor. We duked it out pretty good for a while there, with my Beast getting more punches in than I delivered. He worked me over, but I kept coming back for more. We continued battling for a couple of years before I had finally gained the upper hand – that was, until the day of the Home Invasion.

Disconnected Connection

Much of the unhappiness we experience comes as a result of the actions or choices of those we love. The closer our connection, the more heartbreak or disappointment we can experience. The more we tie our happiness to theirs, the more difficult it can be for us to live happy lives.

There is, perhaps, no greater connection than those we have with our children. A bond exists between a mother or a father, and their child far different from any other type of bond. Since we love our sons and daughters unconditionally and want the best for them, it makes sense that we are happier when their lives are going well.

If their lives take a bad turn, as in the case of Jamie's addiction, it can put us into a tailspin. We jump into "fix-it" mode and do everything we can to try fixing their lives, even at the expense of our own well-being.

We should give advice to our adult children. Even unsolicited advice can often make a difference, even if it is received or acknowledged down the road. We go overboard, however, when our lives are so intertwined with theirs, that we have a hard time finding the separation between them and us.

I saw this all the time with parents when Jamie and Sean were adolescents and teenagers. Helicopter moms had nothing on many of the moms I interacted with; they were more like drone moms. Their children could do no wrong, and they were there to make certain.

When Jamie played competitive softball, there was one drone mom in particular that drove me nuts. She constantly talked about her daughter and her sons as if they were the only kids on the planet. It didn't help that her husband was the coach of the team.

Her daughter, whom I will call, Beth, was an average ballplayer, at best. In her mom's eyes, she was the star of the team. Heck, she was the star of the world. Beth played in the outfield, and often missed, or dropped balls. When this occurred, her mom would yell sweetly,

"It's okay Bethy!"

We should encourage our kids when they make an error in sports since they already feel bad enough and don't need their parents, of all people, making them feel worse. It wasn't what Beth's mom said after she missed a fly ball, or dropped one, it was what she said whenever anyone else did. Maybe I was a tiny bit more sensitive when it was Jamie, but it did seem she was much more vocal on the rare occasion when Jamie didn't make a catch at first base. She would yell in a condescending tone,

"Jamie! You have to make those catches."

It was all I could do to bite my tongue. Half the time I bit it so hard I was sure there was blood dripping down my chin.

Jamie and Sean's best interests were always my top priority, but I was not a helicopter mom, let alone a drone mom. Like most parents, I have never loved, and never will love, anyone else in the way I love my children. At the same time, I was able to see myself as a separate person, but when Jamie's addiction Beast took ahold of her, I had a very hard time separating the two of us.

It was excruciating when I took off what I call my Supermom Cape. Allowing Jamie to walk out her journey, without my intervention took a tremendous amount of courage. For those who are more like Beth's mom, it will be even more difficult than it was for me.

Whether it is your adult child or another person who has caused you to become miserable, it is important you learn to have a disconnected connection. In other words, learn to see yourself as a whole person, separate from your loved one. As long as you stay intertwined with them, unable to separate your purpose from their lives, you could remain stuck, and miserable.

I spent years allowing my happiness to be dependent upon Jamie's journey. Not only did I waste a lot of my precious time, but I can only imagine the extra burden Jamie carried. It was unfair of me to add my happiness to the heavy Beast she was already living with. I allowed my distorted connection to Jamie to keep me from being more fully present in Sean's life. If I were to allow myself regrets, these would be two of them.

It is unrealistic to think our happiness will not be impacted by those we love, but it must not be dependent upon the words or actions of others.

Jamie and I had become physically disconnected, but we have always been spiritually connected. I was finally able to recognize her as a person I loved deeply, but one whose journey was separate from mine. While our lives were intertwined, we were each here for different reasons. This was the disconnected connection that allowed me to find myself again. I stopped adding to her burden and removed the responsibility for my happiness from her shoulders and got on with the business of taking care of my own business. She was never responsible for my happiness anyway.

Miracle Prayer

For years, my first prayer of the morning was for a miracle; for Jamie to stand up and take control of her addiction Beast. Based on her life over the years before I began that prayer, and while I prayed it, I knew it would take a miracle.

I didn't just pray, but I tried hard to believe in the miracle. I would picture Jamie and I having mother-daughter conversations; doing things together. I could see her as a counselor, finally helping others in the way she dreamed of doing. I visualized her telling her story on stage with me, and her writing a book. She would make all of the madness that had become her life, meaningful. This was the "deal" I made with God. I would pray for that miracle every morning, believe it, and one day it would be granted.

Tuesday morning was the first morning after learning of Jamie's death. I only managed to take a few naps during the night, and when I awoke after the final nap, my first thought was the miracle prayer. Instantly I remembered this was not a horrible nightmare. This is a prayer I would never pray again. In the middle of my grief, I laid there confused about what to say to

God, and truthfully, I wasn't even sure I believed in the power of prayer anymore.

I have never thought for a moment that everything we pray for will happen, and in fact, most of the things I have asked for have not come to pass. But, this particular prayer was different. It was the miracle prayer! It was the biggie; the one prayer I would gladly take and forego all of the rest. Now, I was totally confused about prayer.

Worse than my concerns over what to pray about, was the way I was feeling about God. He allowed me to believe for so long that my miracle would come to fruition. While I laid there praying for the miracle each morning, he never let on it was a futile prayer. When I prayed those words, I felt at peace, and that peace is what allowed me to "let her go" for the day. Since I felt such peace and hope about the prayer, I assumed this was a sign from God that the miracle would happen one day.

He failed to give me the "no go" sign. If the miracle prayer was not going to come true, shouldn't God have given me some sort of feeling in the pit of my stomach, rather than allow me to feel peaceful? God let me down and left me feeling like a fool. Could I trust my gut anymore? Could I trust God again?

I know God is ultimately in control of this world, but clearly, he doesn't stop many of the bad things that happen. We live in a world where the Beast is running rampant and one where humans are given free-will to make choices.

Still, God does perform miracles and can stop anything he chooses to stop. If only he would have jammed the gun, or delayed the killer, or caused a series of events to occur, so Jamie would not have been at that house on August 28th, at 9:15 p.m. But he did not. No miracle. I started to think that miracles didn't happen for people like me.

While I prayed for the miracle each morning for years, there was another prayer I only prayed on occasion. It was the one I didn't want to have answered, at least, not if the miracle prayer was still on the table.

As much as I believed in the miracle, there were moments when the gravity of Jamie's life weighed on me; times when I doubted she would make it. On those days I would say the other prayer. It went something like this,

"God, if Jamie is not going to get clean; if she is not going to stand over her Beast, then please take her home."

I only prayed that one a few times; nothing in comparison to the number of times I prayed for the miracle. I had carefully prioritized my requests, so why was it so hard for God to understand which one I really wanted?

After she died, I even reminded him of this, by yelling,

"Don't you understand simple math?"

Obviously, the miracle prayer was the one he should have answered. It was what my heart wanted more than anything. I tried explaining to God that he had gotten this one wrong. I reminded him of all the good Jamie and I could have done together. These were all one-sided discussions.

At that point in my life, I had never walked with so much faith, and I felt as if my reward for the biggest leap of faith I have ever taken, was God pulling the rug out from under me. I was knocked flat on my back, and my Beast got right back on top of me.

It wasn't until I rolled over and got on my knees that I received the answer. The second prayer, the stray prayer I threw in there every now and again when I was feeling overwhelmed with sadness, was the miracle.

God spared Jamie from something worse. Yes, something worse than death. Whatever was up ahead in Jamie's chosen life path was going to be bad – really bad. He spared her from whatever it was.

Rather than allow her family to endure whatever was going to occur, he answered my other prayer. He took Jamie home. She is now safely in the arms of Jesus.

Meanwhile, Back on Planet Earth

Jamie is safe. She is no longer sad or in pain. There is no more choosing between the two lives she was attempting to live. For her, there are no more drugs, health problems, trouble with the law, sadness, or gunshots. There are no more tears. Meanwhile back on planet earth, I was left to figure out how to live without her; to live out the rest of my days with a huge hole in my heart.

A couple of days after Jamie's death, I stood with Sean, his massive arms wrapped around me. He was grieving the loss of his sister, but in those first few days, he was more concerned with making sure I was doing okay.

With my face buried in his chest, sobbing, I asked,

"How am I going to live without her?"

"Because you have another child, Mom; that's how."

He said it matter-of-factly. His voice was calm and caring, but he spoke with such conviction, that I knew it was the truth. This was the moment I knew I would make it, and somehow I could live without Jamie. We would make it together.

LIVING WITH THE HOLE

Those who do not know how to weep with their whole heart don't know how to laugh either.

~ Golda Meir

Before I get into any more of my story or share with you the things that have helped me to go from misery to happiness, I want to acknowledge you. The fact that you picked up this book means you have some hope that you can be happy again. You might feel defeated right now and possibly even think I must have some sort of magical powers that you don't have. I don't. While we all possess very different gifts, talents, wisdom, experiences and perspectives, I don't possess anything you don't already have or that you cannot gain.

Call me crazy, but I am just bold enough to believe YOU are courageous, no matter who you are, or what you are going through. It is in there. It may be hidden underneath all sorts of junk, but it is there. Your Beast may have tried to convince you that you are weak, but he is a liar. I know you are a woman of courage, and I cannot wait for you to believe it too. We are in this together.

Standing with you in love and gratitude,
Valerie

<u>New Normal</u>

The dust was settling; everyone had gone back to their lives, so I had to get on with mine. It was two weeks after Jamie died, and it would be the first time I left the neighborhood by myself.

Driving your car doesn't require a great deal of thought, especially if you have driven it for years, but that first day felt like I was driving a rental car, where every control seems foreign. The route I took was one I had taken many times, yet I had to concentrate on where I was going.

I walked slowly through the grocery store, going through the motions of placing items into my basket. Friends and family had gone home, and we needed some food in the house, but I wasn't hungry and didn't care much about the food I was choosing.

I moved invisibly through the store attempting to make sense of my grocery list. It was as if all of the other people in the store were aware of one another, but nobody saw me. I was in a bubble, moving in my own time and space. Holding back the tears, I labored to make it through this once-familiar task.

I don't recall checking out, or walking back to my car, but somehow I had gotten my groceries into the car and was backing out of the parking stall when suddenly I was on top of the median next to the parking slot. I was shaking as I moved my car off the median and toward the exit. My finger was bleeding pretty badly, but I never did figure out how I had cut it. I wanted to race home and jump into bed, but I made my way to the nail salon.

I was still shaking when I sat down at the table, dreading the look I would see on Kathy's face when I told her about Jamie.

Plus, I didn't want to cry in the nail salon. Before I wrote my first book, I was an emotionally private person and rarely cried in front of anyone. Over the past couple of years, I had made a great deal of progress in allowing myself to show emotion, but the day at the nail salon, I was back to ground zero; trying to pretend everything was okay. In those first weeks and months after Jamie's death, it seemed I reverted to that state many times; trying to act as if I was fine. This typically happened right before I fell apart.

I avoided my office for as long as I could since I didn't have much desire to work, and it made me sad since it was the place I was sitting when I got the knock on the door. When I finally sat at my desk, I felt oddly out of place in front of a computer I had used for years. So, that first day, I lasted about an hour. Slowly I was able to spend more time working again. I changed everything about the room, making it lighter and brighter. It now has many mementos of Jamie that mostly make me smile.

Nothing felt normal anymore: dinners with family and friends, walking to the mailbox, paying bills, cooking, writing, putting on makeup, doing my hair, cleaning, watching television. Nothing felt the same.

I realized all of the activities of my life that had once seemed so normal were not going to feel the same as they did before Jamie died. Nothing would ever be the same again.

I navigated each of the suddenly unfamiliar activities of my life, one by one. It didn't take long for them to begin to feel normal. None of them feel the same as they did before August 28, 2016, but they are normal again; a new normal.

Life has gone on. I sit in the same office as I write this, the same room where I noticed the white SUV in front of the house. It is the same place where I was sitting when I heard my daughter's name as Rich stepped onto the porch and closed the door on that chapter of our lives.

<u>Grief Cyclone</u>

We all experience grief. Unless you love nobody, you will go through it, period. Grief happens after a loss, and nobody is escaping this life without loss.

There is a theory that grief goes through a process of 5 stages: 1) Denial and Isolation; 2) Anger; 3) Bargaining; 4) Depression; and 5) Acceptance.

Having experienced the loss of relationships, marriage, friendships, pets, friends, and family members, I have gone through some or all of these stages, but not in any particular order or process.

While Jamie was alive, I experienced ongoing loss, and therefore ongoing grief. Watching helplessly as someone you love destroys their life, with no end in sight, is a grief I wish nobody had to endure. During those years when Jamie was crashing, I did experience the Five Stages of Grief but in no particular order.

After her death, I have only experienced a couple of those stages. I did have momentary disbelief at times but was never in denial. Okay, maybe when the officer from the coroner's office arrived, and I said "No" about a hundred times. But, I never really went through denial. I only experienced isolation on a few days when I stayed in bed. I never bargained with God. As strange as it seems, I have felt very little anger.

Before I had my first child, women tried to explain to me what labor pains feel like. I read books and tried to imagine how it must feel. My labor pains didn't end up feeling anything like the books explained, or as people tried to describe. It is something you have to experience to fully understand.

It's the same way with losing a child. While it is every parent's worst fear, and most think they could imagine how it would feel, they cannot, and it is not something one can fully describe.

Many parents of addicts will admit they have imagined it, expected it, and perhaps even prayed for their son or daughter to be taken to heaven, to be removed from the addiction nightmare. I did. In those moments, we think we are prepared. There were times when I said, "it wouldn't be better, but it would be easier if God took Jamie home." It turns out there is some truth to that statement, but it doesn't make the hole in my heart any smaller. There is no real way to prepare for the loss of a child, no matter their age or the cause of death.

In my experience, grief does not necessarily go through any sort of process, nor does it follow certain stages. It is more of a

Grief Cyclone. A friend of mine described it as a pair of tennis shoes bouncing around in the dryer.

When the tennis shoes smack me in the face, I allow the grief to come. I acknowledge my loss, and I cry. I grieve, but I just don't stay stuck in my grief.

I met a lady the other day that lost her husband seventeen years ago and is still very much consumed by grief. Many parents have lost their children, and years later they are still paralyzed by grief. I am not judging those people because I know how easy it would be to get swallowed by grief, but I consciously decided this would not be me.

I allow sadness in, and then let it go. Each time, I am stronger afterward. I don't try to cover up the hole in my heart or ignore it. Rather, I accept it as part of my human experience; a reminder of how much I loved Jamie, and still love her. I am learning not to simply live with a hole in my heart, but to embrace it.

Embracing the Hole

Initially, I figured the hole in my heart would shrink until I barely felt it. Over time, Jamie's memory would fade, and little by little, I would stop missing her. While it has only been just over a year since her death, I am convinced that I will always miss her.

The hole left by a loved one might shrink over time, but it doesn't ever completely heal. One created by the loss of a child doesn't shrink at all. I will live out my days in full awareness of the hole.

This is the price we pay for loving our children. Although one half of Jamie's thirty-year life was unimaginable, I would do it all over again. I would not have wanted to miss the opportunity to be Jamie's mom and to experience all that she was.

When overwhelming sadness comes, I embrace it. I allow myself to grieve; to go to the sad place where the hole exists. I just don't remain there for very long.

Once I understood the relationship I would continue to have with the hole in my heart, it has made my grieving process more acceptable. I don't fight it. Rather, I allow it to be a constant reminder of how blessed I am to have loved someone as fiercely as I loved Jamie. While I would rather have been able to love her in the physical sense for the rest of my life, I can accept that I won't.

The hole in my heart will ache at times. The tears will flow. When the tears stop, I put a smile on my face and remember what an incredible gift I was given.

Choosing Memories

It doesn't seem as if we can choose our memories. After all, they randomly appear in our minds. I have been driving down the road and had some scenes from three or four decades past pop into my head. A certain song can bring memories flooding back. A smell can propel us into the past in an instant.

Having said that I also know we can control most of our thoughts, and therefore much of the memories we allow to take up space in our heads.

I remember vividly picking Jamie up several years ago on Thanksgiving, completely high out of her mind. I will never forget seeing her lying in the hospital with a breathing tube in her mouth. I can recall in an instant the last Christmas we were together, the last time I saw her trying to pretend she wasn't using again. I have all sorts of unhappy memories, but I choose not to think about them.

It's not that I am burying my head in the sand, but what good are those memories? Would it help me to picture her last moment on earth; the instant she realized she was about to die? It wouldn't change one single thing about what happened, but allowing the negative, heartbreaking memories in, or imagining her death will keep me trapped in grief, and living as a victim.

Continuing to replay those memories would mean Jamie's legacy is one of sadness and tragedy. Instead, I remember Jamie for the incredible person she was. I recall her humor and quick wit; how she lit up a room.

My niece, Shawnie, and Jamie were the best of friends until all hell broke loose. During the last half of Jamie's life, they became somewhat estranged, but the few times they did get together, it seemed as if no time had passed between them. I can still hear the laughter of this dynamic duo.

Shawnie's parents divorced when she was very young, and her mom remarried. Shawnie has a brother, Shane, from that marriage. Just over a month before Jamie was killed, Shawnie's brother died very unexpectedly. As you can imagine, Shawnie was devastated by the loss of her brother, and then the second blow of losing her precious cousin. Those few weeks changed Shawnie's life forever, but I am proud of my niece for navigating this period of her life in the manner she is choosing. She is taking the two holes in her heart and using them to help her find her purpose. Shawnie is doing her best to honor the memories of her brother and her cousin, and to keep those good memories alive.

Yesterday morning, she sent this email to a few of us who were closest to Jamie:

Good Morning,

I dreamt of Jamie last night and wanted to share with you all. It was nothing too eventful, but it was perfect. All I remember is we were at a family gathering, Jamie was happy and healthy. We were probably around 20 years old. She and I were two peas in a pod hanging together, laughing at how funny and crazy our big family was. Maybe even feeling a little 'too cool for school.' All of the usual things that made up the Jamie and Shawnie show. ☺

Randomly, I remember there were puppies that we were playing with (golden retrievers) and babies. Many books I have read on people experiencing Heaven, such as the one about the little boy, Heaven is For Real, talk about babies and children being there. And of course, we know, All Dogs Go to Heaven.

Although not what I would necessarily call a "visitation dream," I do know that any dream where I get to spend time with Jamie is special, and a cherished gift. This really proves that we don't necessarily remember everything someone said to us, but it is how they made us feel that is special and forever a part of who we are.

Love you all. Love you, Jamie.

Shawnie

The more we carefully choose our memories, the more of those types of positive and uplifting memories become our subconscious thoughts.

Shawnie's dream could have left her feeling sad that she is not going to see Jamie again in this lifetime, and I am certain she did feel some sadness, but she is choosing to cherish her memories of Jamie. She is choosing how those memories make her feel.

We can control our thoughts, and therefore our memories, and even our feelings. You can choose what you think about, so choose to recall good times. Choose to picture your loved one vibrant and happy. Choose to replay fun times. Choose to laugh about a funny memory. Choose your memories carefully.

I choose to remember Jamie's laugh, her smile, and her sense of humor. I remember so many funny little things she said or did. I remember how much she loved her family and friends, children and pets. I choose to remember her love and acceptance of others and how she didn't judge people. I remember her hug. I choose to remember her in her little softball uniform scooping up balls at first base. I remember how she always called me, "mommy." I love how we kept saying "Lubadoo" instead of "I love you too" — something she said when she first learned to speak. I choose my memories.

Using the "F" Word In a Big Way

Over the years I have seen news reports or television specials where parents of homicide victims openly forgave the killer. I recall thinking how amazing that was, but not something I could do if someone killed my child.

These must be special people right up there with the anointed saints. They were probably preacher's kids, or pastors themselves. They were likely raised in strong church homes. They were chosen by God to know how to do all of the super high-level forgiving stuff. They were the kind of people who were born at peace. They were not people like me.

I have since fallen in love with the "F" word. I use it everywhere and with as many people as possible. I forgave Jamie, her dad, family and friends, the people she was hanging out with, and even myself. I forgave the friend who brought her drugs in rehab and her boyfriend who helped her to stay in her addiction. I forgave the guy who shot her back in 2004.

I was really onto something with this forgiveness thing. I liked using the "F" word. It seemed I could forgive pretty much anyone for anything. Then somebody took my daughter's life. Suddenly I was in a position of needing to forgive a guy who had murdered

59

Jamie and had yet to be held accountable. This guy was going about his life while I tried to figure out how to live without my daughter.

It wasn't fair. It wasn't right. It wasn't the way life was supposed to go. It wasn't something that should happen to me. It wasn't a lot of things, but it was now my reality.

Was I going to be able to use the "F" word on a cold-blooded murderer? I wanted to use the "F" word on him alright, but it was a completely different "F" word, and I am sure it was used on him a few times.

I understood God wanted me to forgive this person; we had already been down this road after the first shooting. I knew firsthand how anger could eat me up on the inside, but this time my daughter was gone. There cannot be things much worse than losing a child, so nobody would blame me if I never forgave the killer. In fact, many people would expect me not to forgive him.

Especially in these situations, such as the murder of a loved one, it can seem next to impossible even to consider forgiving someone, let alone actually doing it. The horrific nature of such a thing leaves us feeling justified in not forgiving. It is easier to forgive people for small things, but for something like murder; it's a pretty big leap.

What gets in the way is our confusion between forgiveness and justice. It is so unfair that Jamie is gone and at the time of publication of this book, no arrests have been made. No justice has been served. However, there is a big difference between forgiveness and justice. I want justice for Jamie, and for this guy to be taken off the streets before he has a chance to hurt more people, but I decided very early on that I am not in the justice business. I have to leave it to law enforcement and the justice system. I have to leave it to God.

So, I have forgiven that guy. Whoever he is, and wherever he is, he is forgiven. I must repeat – I do want justice. Please don't confuse the two.

If there ever is a trial and I face my daughter's murderer, I will publicly forgive him. I have even pictured embracing his mother, as I can only imagine how hard it will be for her.

I have done something I could never have imagined. You probably think it has been hard to do, but it hasn't. If you had told me years ago my precious girl would be murdered and asked me if I would be able to forgive her killer, I am certain I would have answered with an emphatic, "no" and perhaps a "hell no," but I was a different person back then. I used to believe, as most people do, that someone has to deserve forgiveness in order for us to give it. I now understand the truth - forgiveness is for the person doing the forgiving. It releases us from the hold another person's actions or words have over us. It removes anger and resentment.

This guy took the irreplaceable from me. He blew a permanent hole in my heart. That's enough. I will not give him more of my life. He took a piece of my heart, and I won't surrender any more of it.

We have to stop acting as if we are doing others a favor by forgiving them. The forgiveness is not for them. It is for us. We should let God deal with the people who have hurt us.

Don't use the "F" word because they deserve forgiveness; use it because you deserve peace.

Signs, Signs, Everywhere a Sign

Often after the death of a loved one, it is hard to find much peace. This is especially the case when we lose children or in the case of a sudden or tragic death. We are left with this gaping wound in our hearts, and the world seems upside down. We question God's goodness, and we wonder how to continue on without the connection we once knew.

Death is permanent, but only in the physical sense. Our souls are eternal, and our connection to the people we love doesn't die when their bodies leave this earth.

I knew right away Jamie was in heaven, but I needed the comfort of a sign. I had been praying, more like begging, for a sign from God that not only was Jamie with him but still with me.

Often, we think God will only speak to us in our prayers, or at church. Maybe he only sends messages through spiritual leaders. We tend to forget God has dominion over everything and can send us a sign in any way, and through whomever or whatever he chooses.

Seriously, Birds?

It was a big deal. I was leaving the house for the first time. I was only walking to the mailbox, but it was a big deal. It was three days after Jamie's death.

I was open to recognizing one of those signs from Jamie that I had been hoping and praying for, but I certainly was not expecting one on the way to the mailbox.

Heading down my street, I noticed two birds flying fairly low, and directly overhead. Birds flying overhead are not exactly a newsworthy event or even a sign. I have seen lots of birds flying together, often in a flock, or flying in some pattern. I have even seen two birds flying together.

What I had never seen before or since was what I saw that day. Two birds flew together in perfect unison, side-by-side, with their wings nearly touching. It was reminiscent of the near-perfect unison of the Navy's Blue Angels that I saw fly over Lake Washington in Seattle each August, during Sea Fair.

I watched the two birds until they were out of sight, and they never broke formation. As long as my eye could see them, they flew side by side, their wings nearly touching. Me and Jamie, still side by side.

Again with the Birds?

My brother Brad was in town, and it was nearly two weeks after Jamie died.

The first couple of days he was here, I stayed in my room a lot. He's the kind of guy that does his own thing, so he was fine with it. It was actually wonderful having him here after others had left because he knows how to just "be."

One day I was lying on my bed watching television, where I had been the entire day. Brad walked into my room, looked at the television and said,

"I love Property Brothers."

He got onto the bed next to me and started watching. He didn't ask how I was doing, or anything. He just laid with me, commenting on the show. It was a perfect hour.

The next day he asked me to go on a short hike with him. Hiking is something I always loved and spent years doing when I lived in the Seattle area. I have hiked a little bit around Palm Springs, but haven't found any serious hiking friends yet, and Rich is much more of a golfer than a hiker. I was reluctant to leave the house, but off we went.

As we headed back down the trail, Brad told me he was looking for a special spot to pay tribute to Jamie. He hadn't told anyone of his plan. This is how Brad operates, and that day I was glad it was a spontaneous moment.

We sat together in silence on the top of some boulders quite aways off the trail.

Suddenly, my brother said,

"Look at that hummingbird trying to get your attention."

It darted close to me, flew away and then shot back toward me. It did this a few times, and as we watched, it flew about fifteen feet away and settled on a small bush. It then turned its tiny head toward us, exposing a deep fuchsia colored neck and chest. Pink was Jamie's favorite color.

I have seen plenty of hummingbirds, but to this day, I have never seen one this color.

While birds can be beautiful and fascinating, I don't particularly like them or want them to touch me. I always believed God has a sense of humor, but sending me two messages via bird antics makes it certain.

The Perfect Half Moon

I have always loved the moon. We had a children's book about the moon that I read to Jamie and Sean over and over, never certain who enjoyed the book more, them or me.

One evening when they were young, I took them to a spot where they could get an awesome view of a Supermoon. All of my excitement was lost on them, but I thought it was magnificent! I'm not sure what my fascination is with the moon, but God understands.

A couple of months after Jamie died, I noticed the moon was full, but in those days I was not as excited about the moon as I normally am, so I didn't think much about it.

One early morning a few days later, I was out walking when I looked up into the dawn sky. There sat the faint outline of a near perfect half-moon. I could just make out the semi-circle of the moon's other half. My sign that Jamie and I are forever connected.

The Dreams

My dreams are very real. Now and then Rich will have a dream, and he will try to express just how real this dream was. He might even say,

"This one was so real; it was in full color!"

I stand there looking at him perplexed. ALL of my dreams are in full color, and very real. I have never had a black and white dream; although I think it might be pretty cool. My dreams are so real that it often takes me some time after waking to shake the feeling the events didn't actually occur.

I had a very vivid Jamie dream. As I said, my dreams are real, but this dream was different. In all of my other dreams, the setting is never exactly as it is, or as it ever was. Often, they will take place in a home where I have lived, but many things will be different about the home. Or, it will be in a house that I know is my home in the dream, but not one I have ever lived in. In this particular dream, everything in the living room of my current home is exactly as it was in the dream, a home Jamie never stepped foot into. It was the most real dream I have ever had, and that is saying something.

Jamie appeared in the living room, sitting on the coffee table directly in front of me. I took her face in my hands and kissed her repeatedly, telling her how much I loved and missed her. I asked her how it could be possible she was sitting right there.

She smiled her big beautiful smile and said,

"I'm right here mommy."

When I awoke, I knew the dream was special. Jamie had visited me. This was another sign Jamie is still right here.

During one of the very long periods when I didn't see Jamie or hear from her, I told Rich,

"I am starting to forget her."

I could no longer hear Jamie's voice, no matter how quiet I got, or how hard I tried. Our VHS home movie archives had been mistakenly recorded over the top of, and since Jamie was in and out of our lives for nearly half of hers, I didn't have any recent videos or voice recordings. Not being able to hear her voice in my head upset me. When Jamie died suddenly, I realized once again, that I could not hear her voice. I tried and tried, but I could not recall it. This shook me up.

Shortly after this realization, I had another dream. I was in a house I had never seen, but knew to be mine, when the phone rang.

I heard Jamie's voice.

"Mommy?"

"Jamie! Oh my God, is this you?"

"It's me mommy; you know my voice." It was her "silly mom" tone she often took.

"But, I thought you were…dead." I was almost afraid to say it, hoping it wasn't true.

"I'm right here, mom. I don't have much time, though. I just want you to know I'm okay, but we will never be able to see each other or talk again. I just wanted you to know I am okay and that I love you."

"No! Jamie, where are you? I want to see you. Please, tell me where you are."

"Mommy, it has to be this way. Please don't tell anyone, not even Rich."

"Jamie, please, just tell me where you are; I want to see you!"

"I have to go now."

"No, Jamie, please don't go!"

"Bye, Mommy. I love you."

"I love you, Jamie!"

The phone disconnected.

While Jamie didn't say so, it was understood in the conversation that she was in witness protection.

Although my brother Brad offered to come down and identify Jamie's body, we chose not to have anyone go through that ordeal. The morning I awoke from the dream, I panicked. What if she really had been placed in witness protection and the ashes we had yet to spread were not hers! Between the positive identification of the coroner, the news reports where Jamie's picture was shown, Facebook posts from her friends, and those who contacted us, we knew it really was Jamie. Still, it took me a few hours to get back to reality. It was only a dream.

I like to make sense of things, so I wanted to make sense of this dream. I do believe many dreams help us to process, and some can be signs, but I have had far too many that made absolutely no sense, to believe all dreams have a specific meaning. I let it go and put it into the "weird dream" category.

But something else happened the day after this particular dream. It was the first day in weeks that I could hear her voice again. I can still hear it today.

A Butterfly Returns

My friend Penny sent some live Monarch butterflies shortly after Jamie's death. We had no memorial planned yet, and the butterflies needed to be released right away, so Rich and I had a private butterfly release ceremony.

We opened thirty-six individual envelopes, each printed:

Jamie Lynn

August 28, 2016

Some of the butterflies fluttered their wings and took to flight immediately after we opened the envelopes. Others took a few seconds longer to awake, and some had to be placed on the ground, needing extra time. Eventually, many of the butterflies fluttered to nearby bushes or trees. Some flew away, and a couple didn't make it. It was a very special time and such a beautiful symbol of Jamie's freedom from her Beast.

A month or so later, I was exercising in my backyard. I love to be outside, so I even do as many workouts as I can outdoors. One of my regular workouts is interval training, where I do a series of squats, lunges, and light hand weights. There is a putting green in our side yard, so I will often do parts of this work out on that side of the house. It happens to be where Rich and I let the butterflies go. On one particular day, I was lunging down the length of the putting green when a Monarch butterfly fluttered around my head and then settled on a plant about ten feet from me.

I started to talk to the butterfly as if it were Jamie. It might sound as if I was losing it, but I talk to Jamie out loud often. Had you been there, it probably wouldn't have seemed as crazy as it does as I type this.

I lunged closer to the butterfly expecting her to fly off. Yes, I choose to believe it was a girl butterfly, as I couldn't get close enough to check. She stayed put while I went about my workout and attempted to converse with her. No matter how close I got to the plant, she remained there.

After a while, I stopped talking to the butterfly. See, I am not completely crazy. When I did, she came toward me, and fluttered around my head, before settling back on the plant. I could get as close as I wanted, and she just sat there, but if I ignored her for too long, she would flutter over to me and get my attention. A lot like Jamie.

I spent about ten or fifteen minutes with my Jamie butterfly, grateful for another sign that my girl is still with me.

The Cloud of Witnesses

Recently, I spoke at an event late in the afternoon on the final day. Following my message a line formed at my book table, and I spent most of the break talking with people. For a few moments toward the end of the break, I sat alone gathering my thoughts. It was the only moment I recall being completely by myself the entire weekend. A sweet blonde woman approached me with a note in her hand. She explained she was leaving and had written the note expecting to slip it to me on her way out. Since she caught me alone, she asked if she could read it to me.

We sat together as she lovingly read me the note while tears streamed down my face:

Dear Valerie,

Thank you for sharing your story today! I want to share with you a vision I had. I saw a beautiful young lady in the "cloud of witnesses," who very clearly said to you,

"Mommy, it is well with my soul."

It was a beautiful moment, and I sensed that she was living her dream in heaven. I also heard,

"Thank you for praying for me."

Bless you, Valerie, you have blessed my heart with your story.

~ Trish

A couple days later, my sister-in-law was visiting, and we stopped at Hobby Lobby. They have a few household items displayed in the foyer just outside the store entrance. Suzanne pointed out a couple of crosses leaning on a shelf and immediately I saw it. It was this cross, with the same words Trish had shared, "It is well with my soul." It is a turquoise color, perfect for where it hangs in my house.

When you go through the grieving process after losing a loved one, you may or may not notice any signs. We cannot be one hundred percent certain my experiences were messages from God, or a sign sent to remind me Jamie is with me, but I believe they were.

Whether or not they were, there is no doubt we see signs from God every single day. Every smile from a stranger, each sunrise, the beauty of nature, babies, the laughter of a child, the devotion of our pets, the gift of family and friends, and the opportunity to make a difference, are sure signs from the creator of the universe.

So, I choose to believe God uses dreams, people, and even birds to let us know our loved ones are safe and they continue to live in our hearts. You can't force these signs to occur, but you need to be open to the possibility; to keep your eyes and heart open so you don't miss them.

<u>Peace That Surpasses My Understanding</u>

For decades I envied people who somehow found the peace that surpasses all understanding; those who seemed to be at peace even in the midst of hardship and loss. They had peace when life had taken an unfair turn. They stayed peaceful when a situation was out of control. They found peace after incredible heartbreak.

Even before all hell broke loose, it didn't seem likely I would ever be that type of person. It didn't fit my personality. After I met my Beast, I stopped even imagining this type of peace; it was far beyond my reach.

A few years back I went on my Frantic Quest For Peace. This may sound like an oxymoron, but it perfectly describes my desire for peace and my willingness to find it. When I prayed for myself, I began to pray for peace more than anything else. It is what I desired day in and day out while my life was filled with chaos and uncertainty.

It was apparent the storm was not going to cease anytime soon, so I boldly stepped up to the heavenly plate and asked for peace in the middle of it, and I received it.

Just over a year after Jamie's unsolved murder, and sixteen years after all hell broke loose, I feel incredible peace. Truthfully, now and then a small part of me wonders if the peace is just going to evaporate one day; disappear as quickly as it arrived.

People ask about the status of Jamie's case and then go on to comment on how hard it must be to live with her murderer on the loose, but it isn't. I know this makes absolutely no sense – it hardly makes sense to me.

I am not sure if my sense of peace is the peace that surpasses "all" understanding, but it certainly is a peace that surpasses "my" understanding.

You should pray for peace, but there is more to this than simply praying. Here is the key to receiving peace - you must stop living in chaos and drama. The choices you make each day will determine how quickly, or if, you will ever find that state of peace. God will do his part, but we have to meet him somewhere on the road to peace.

"Turn from evil and do good; seek peace and pursue it."

~ Psalm 34:14

CHOOSE HAPPINESS

A woman in harmony with her spirit is like a river flowing. She goes where she will without pretense, and arrives at her destination prepared to be herself and only herself.

~ Maya Angelou

Misery Happens

Remember the bumper sticker that simply said, "Shit happens?" Some would rather say, "Stuff happens." The point is that things happen for which we have no control. In other words, life happens. As a result, misery happens too.

Children don't come into the world in a state of misery. We become miserable as the events of our lives unfold. Misery takes ahold of us during or after hardship, massive disappointment, heartbreak, or loss. Put another way - life happens. Without working to overcome misery, we get stuck there.

Webster Dictionary defines "misery" as 1) a state of suffering and want that is the result of poverty or affliction; 2) a circumstance, thing, or place that causes suffering or discomfort; and 3) a state of great unhappiness and emotional distress.

We have all been miserable at times. I was miserable during some of my first marriage. There were periods of misery sprinkled throughout my childhood and into adulthood. None of my prior bouts of misery compared to the near-constant state of misery I lived in during my thirteen-year ride on my Roller Coaster From Hell. I got on the ride as a result of my daughter's addiction and all of the drama, chaos, disappointment, heartbreak, and fear that comes with addiction. You became miserable due to the events in your life.

I was tempted to return to a miserable state after losing Jamie, and even more so as the days, weeks, and months passed with no justice for her murder.

It is easy to become a miserable person focusing on everything that is wrong. Life rarely goes as we had hoped, wished, or even planned. The easy way out is to become cynical, negative and miserable.

Most people don't want to be miserable, but they don't know how to stop. Yes, there are certain people who do appear to enjoy being miserable, but I doubt most of them are enjoying it as much as they pretend to be.

Misery happens, but you don't have to stay that way.

<u>Victimland</u>

Disneyland is a theme park divided into eight different lands. Among them, you can visit Tomorrowland or Fantasyland. What you will not find in the "happiest place on earth," is Victimland.

In Victimland, you will be surrounded by like-minded people, so initially, this might seem like a magical place, but unlike lands at Disneyland, Victimland is far from happy. There is only one ride, and it is the Roller Coaster From Hell. The good news is that you get a guide on the singular ride in Victimland. The bad news is the guide will be your Beast.

Music is played throughout the land; songs of sadness, loss, loneliness, and fear.

There are several movie theaters strategically placed around the property, and they are open 24/7. You can pop into a theater without the need for a ticket and watch as the sad moments of your life repeat themselves on the big screen. If you get tired of watching your own story, you need only to move to another theater to watch a series of depressing movies from the lives of other inhabitants of Victimland.

Shame hangs in the air over this land, like a dense fog. The soot of guilt settles over everything and everyone. Day after day, another layer of shame covers the people of Victimland until their skin is thick with shame and guilt.

This is a place where nobody tries to "one-up" the other by telling stories that are bigger than the last. Rather, they are intent on "one-downing" each other. Each story becomes more depressing than the last.

The longer you live in Victimland, the more confused you become. It was such a comforting place when you first arrived, but you feel lonelier and sadder than the day you got there. Gone is your hope of being happy again. Joy is a distant memory.

You no longer look forward to seeing the people you once were so thankful to have found. Now, even though you are still surrounded by people who understand your story, you have never felt so alone.

Becoming a victim may not have been your fault, but remaining one is your choice. Living your life as a victim will keep you hopeless and helpless. There is zero power in Victimland. Nobody is happy there. Nobody is living courageously.

Stand up and claim your place as a victor. Cross back over the border, out of Victimland, and never look back.

The Little Thing That Changes Everything

Positive thinking and having a positive mindset or attitude is nothing new. It is, however, a powerful ability few seem to take advantage of.

Thoughts precede the actions we take, and the words we speak, even though it seems many people speak without thinking. Whether our words come from conscious or subconscious thoughts, it all starts with our thinking. In a nutshell, thoughts dictate what we say and do, so our thoughts have tremendous power.

Consider two people with similar circumstances, and if you were to watch their daily life, it would appear as if the one with the positive attitude did not have the same problems as the one with the negative attitude.

A particular situation may not immediately change just because you adopt a positive mindset, but having the right attitude can make your life appear as if many things have changed.

I was hesitant to call a good attitude a "little thing" as the title of this chapter suggests but chose to do so because it is one thing that can be changed immediately. It is a seemingly little thing that can have a huge impact.

87

I wrote a post on my Facebook page about perspective. It was after my husband's surgery and the delays that happened that day. It was also the day after the horrific event in Las Vegas, Nevada when nearly sixty people died, and hundreds were injured at the hands of a madman. In reply, Christina posted this message:

> *Thank you for your post! I have been following you for quite some time and have worked through your book and workbook. My daughter was addicted to heroin and is now thankfully, 3 years clean. You have been a Godsend and such a help to me, and I wanted to thank you.*
>
> *Unfortunately we just lost a daughter-in-law in the Las Vegas tragedy and again are faced with heartache but you have taught me to be strong in the storm. Thank you again for all you do and I will continue to follow your work and mission to help others battle their Beast!!*

Christina was not only suffering heartbreak and loss, but it was a front-page news story so it would have been expected that her first words would have been about her connection to the tragedy. Yet, Christina wrote first of her gratitude. She closed her message with more gratitude and with determination to keep standing. Christina exemplifies a person using the power of a *little* thing called attitude.

You can change your attitude immediately, but keeping a good attitude will take practice. Having a negative, cynical, or doomsday attitude becomes a habit. You will have to kick the habit. It will be a conscious effort to switch out the thoughts you have with new ones; to look for things that are good in your life. See things not-so-good things in a new light.

Having the right attitude no matter what is happening is a key component to happiness. Far too many are looking to outside influences, circumstance, or other people to make them happy. If you want to be happy, I mean truly happy, take a long hard look at the attitude you embrace each day.

"Optimists can often be wrong,
but they are happy and wrong."
~ Sue Fitzmaurice

<u>Gaining Perspective</u>

I have had three repeating dreams in my life. One of them, I don't like to talk about because those dreams were so disturbing.

When Sean was young, I had repeating dreams that he was drowning, and I couldn't save him. One time, we were at a pool, and he was struggling to stay afloat, and I could not get to him. Another time, we were on a cruise ship, and he fell overboard. The circumstances of each dream were different, but each was distressing.

It was odd because Sean took swimming lessons at an early age, and knew how to swim. He had never been in a situation when he was in danger of drowning. I believe this dream represented my big fear that something would happen to one of my kids. I used to say if anything happened to one of them, I would be "done." I would be balled up in a corner rocking back and forth, unable to function. Well, something did happen to one of mine, and I am not "done."

When imagining something bad happening, especially to someone you love, there is an overwhelming feeling you wouldn't be able to handle whatever it is. When all hell breaks loose, you discover you can handle a whole lot more than ever imagined, more than you ever wanted to imagine. You also gain some interesting perspective.

At age 15, one week after bible camp, Jamie was arrested for shoplifting at our local mall. The phone call took my breath away. Seriously – I was hyperventilating. I thought it was the worst day of my life. I was horrified that *my daughter,* one who had been raised by the honesty police had done such a thing.

Now I nearly laugh at how devastated I was. Don't get me wrong, shoplifting isn't funny, but after what I have endured, my reaction to the shoplifting event is somewhat comical. I certainly would not have wanted Jamie to become a serial shoplifter, but I wish that was as bad as it got.

I cannot even describe how I felt the time Jamie had to wear an ankle bracelet to avoid being in jail. Surely *this* was as bad as it would get. At least she wasn't in jail.

The first time Jamie went to jail, I cried continuously for seven hours straight. Nothing ever came of the arrest, but I couldn't bear the thought of *my daughter* sitting in jail. The situation had something to do with the people she called friends, and it was an opportunity for a good lesson for Jamie, but I didn't care. I did not want my daughter in jail! My husband wanted to leave her there over the weekend and let her get out at the hearing on Monday, but I couldn't handle it. Repeatedly, I cried,

"I can't have my daughter in jail. I can't."

You would think I was the one in jail! Very reluctantly, Rich agreed to bail her out, mainly because I pressured him, and he was tired of hearing me cry. Plus, I made sure he understood how hard this was for me and that he didn't understand because he was her step-father. When she was lying in the hospital with a bullet in her gut, I would have opted for her sitting in jail for the weekend. The next couple of times she went to jail, I was relieved.

In the early years of Jamie's addiction, I thought the pain and disappointment would kill me, if not physically, then certainly emotionally. My heart was broken, standing helplessly as Jamie moved deeper into the belly of her Beast.

If I had ever imagined all of this, I am sure I would not have thought I could survive it all. At each stage of the process, I thought it was the worst thing I could endure.

When you think you cannot make it through whatever it is you are currently dealing with, it is helpful to recall how far you have come. It is likely you are surprised by some of the things you have made it through already. Looking back, it may seem as if some of the experiences you never thought you would survive, are nothing compared to what you are dealing with now.

You handled far more than you could have imagined, and you can handle more. After all, your record for making it through these tough times so far is 100%. This may not bring you much comfort as you would probably rather not have to face the things that might occur in your future, but if they are coming your way, wouldn't you rather be prepared for them?

Life is tough. We are all going to face challenges and trials. This is a fact of life, so rather than running from our problems, we should gain as much courage as we can, so the things we face won't destroy us. The more courageous you become, the more you will be able to handle things you once thought impossible.

<u>Shedding the Shame</u>

I have never had trouble laughing at myself or admitting when I have messed up. In fact, I can be downright self-deprecating, for the sake of humor. Shame is something else.

"I'm ashamed of you."

"You should be ashamed of yourself."

We have heard those stinging words, and we have probably said them. Parents often use these terms as a way to correct behavior. When a child lies or steals, these words are meant to have a lasting impact. When we were told by our parents that our behavior was shameful, we paid attention.

When I was eleven years old, my friend Karen stole a candy bar from our local grocery store. I didn't know she had done it, but when I saw the candy, I wanted one too. We didn't have much money, so candy was a luxury. We went back to the store so I could get my candy bar. Obviously, I was not much of a criminal mastermind.

We walked around the side of the store toward the path that led to our neighborhood, happily eating the candy bars, when we heard shouting behind us. We turned to find the mean red-haired lady from the store, walking toward us. My heart was beating out of my chest as I started walking toward her, breaking up the candy bar behind me as I did. Apparently, the mean lady was too focused on the evidence Karen held in her hands to notice the candy trail behind me.

We were hauled into the store, and Karen's mom was called. My mom was not notified because I had only been an accomplice. My mom was not friends with Karen's mom, so I knew they wouldn't talk about the incident, and I was safe in telling my mom Karen had stolen the candy bar, and I was simply guilty of being with her. The only reason I had to tell my mom at all is that we were both banned from the store; the same one where I shopped with my mom every week.

I was terrified to face my mom, so instead, I wrote her a note. Years later she showed me the note, and it wasn't until I read it again that I realized how much of the story I had purposely omitted. I finally confessed the whole truth, and I was actually glad it had come up again because the stupid decision to steal the candy bar was one I regretted.

My mom didn't say anything to me after she got the note; instead, she barely said a word to me for about two weeks! It was worse than being on restriction, getting yelled at, or even being told how ashamed she was of me. The look of shame said it all and the silence was deafening. I never did steal anything again, so perhaps, in that case, the shame was effective.

Somehow I managed to make it out of childhood without a thick layer of shame covering me, but others did not. They continue to wear the shame their entire lives.

We live in an age where too many people are not willing to accept responsibility for their actions or words, so I am not suggesting we give people a free pass. We need to own up to our mistakes and choices.

At the same time, we need more grace and forgiveness. When someone has made poor choices, they live with shame. We can even take on the shame of our loved ones.

When my fears became a reality, and Jamie finally admitted she was addicted to drugs, I was devastated. What I didn't realize is the Beast had begun painting me with shame. As Jamie's ride on her Roller Coaster From Hell continued, she spent time in jail, participated in illegal activities, became friends with drug dealers and gang members, and more. She didn't seem to find much wrong with her actions, at least it was the persona she portrayed. I was ashamed of Jamie, and I transferred that shame to me. A layer of shame was painted over me like a second skin.

I was the mom of an addict. There was no way out and no way to spin this one. There was no way to make sense of it or to reconcile my parenting to what was happening. I was now "one of those parents." My Beast took out the paint brush and slathered on the shame.

I didn't have to spend much time wondering what other people were thinking of me as a parent. For years, I had plenty to say about "those parents" whose children became addicts, or criminals, so I knew what they were likely thinking. The more I realized what people were thinking, the thicker the layers of shame grew.

One of the Beast's favorite tactics is shame. If we remain covered with shame, it is unlikely we will ever stand up and use our story to make a difference. Shame keeps us isolated. Isolation keeps the shame intact. Around and around we go. Not being able to live in the truth of our past, of our entire story, will keep us from true happiness.

At some point, I started to avoid the whole Jamie subject. If someone asked about my kids, I told them I had a son. Sometimes I was simply too tired to get into it, but often it was my shame that kept me from mentioning Jamie.

Once I came out of my cave; my self-imposed prison of depression, shame, and fear, the most amazing thing began to happen. I stopped avoiding the Jamie discussion, and people started to tell their stories. More often than not when they watched the matter of fact way I spoke, they opened up, and I would hear about addiction affecting them, or someone close to them. I could see the relief on their faces and hear the connection in their voices.

There are times when the stories I hear have nothing to do with addiction, but people feel safe to share their stories because I share mine without shame.

The more I was open about my life, my Beast, and Jamie's, the less shame I felt. The less shame, the more I stayed out of my cave. The less isolation I allowed in my life, the more I realized I was not alone. The more connection I had with others, the more the shame melted from me. Before long, I was standing on top of my story; living without shame.

Stop slinking into support meetings, afraid to state your full name. Don't hide your story from family and friends. The first steps in shedding your shame need to come from you. You might be surprised how people will react when you own your story. Some of the people you think you are hiding it from might know anyway. If others don't accept you, judge you, or look down on you because of your past or current situation, you might need to move on.

Shame begets shame, and the cycle continues. It stops when you say it stops. I say it stops now.

"Never bend your head. Always hold it high. Look the

world straight in the eye."

~ Helen Keller

<u>Giving Up the Guilt</u>

Back in my shame and guilt days, I had a very hard time accepting that I was not somehow responsible for Jamie's addiction. It wasn't just that I had stood on my soapbox condemning parents whose sons and daughters were living the life Jamie was living, but there had to be a reason for her addiction. It could not simply be that she had a predisposition for addiction as her dad did. It couldn't have been her choice. There had to be something – big. Some decision I made, something I didn't give her as a child. It had to be about me.

At some point in my journey, I knew deep down I was not at fault, but I couldn't seem to shake the guilt I felt. I kept apologizing to God over and over. He gave Jamie to *me*, and I should have done a better job of parenting. My head kept telling me it was not my fault, but my heart was saying God must think I am a failure. Jamie was gifted with more raw talent, intelligence, and character than anyone I knew. Surely, that was by design. She was supposed to go out into the world and make a difference in a big way. From where I sat, that was not happening. Not even close.

I repeatedly apologized to God for messing up one of his precious souls; one he entrusted to me. Finally, a friend helped me to understand a new perspective when she said,

"It's not all about you."

If it was not all about me, then who was it about? Oh yeah, that's right – Jamie. Sure, it affected me. It nearly destroyed me, but this was Jamie's journey to travel.

I made mistakes, and so did Jamie. We all do. It was time to forgive myself; time to stop making this all about me.

After she was killed, I couldn't help but wonder if I should have started chasing after her again and somehow made her get clean. In our last email communication, she voiced her desire to be with her family and even said life without us was not much of a life. I did tell her I would stand with her and even offered up something for treatment. But, I didn't chase her. For that, I felt the familiar pangs of guilt. As the murder investigation grows colder, the guilt sometimes tries to creep in, but I fight it. I gave up guilt a long time ago.

It is time for you to give up your guilt. Stop punishing yourself. You are not proving anything to anyone by beating yourself up. The only thing you are accomplishing is not accepting the invitation to live in freedom.

Refusing the Stigma

Stigma surrounds many things.

A young adult makes a bad decision and winds up with a felony on their record. No matter how much their life turns around, that mistake follows them like a black mark. He's a criminal.

So many other things have a stigma attached to them, resulting in shame, guilt, and isolation.

She's got mental problems.

He's an addict, junkie, loser, weak-willed.

They are divorced.

She's the mom with the kid who is addicted to heroin.

It's the last example I can relate to. Society as a whole has been pretty sure either an addict got that way because they are weak-willed, or because they have bad parents.

One's will can have something to do with whether or not they seek treatment, or how hard they fight, but there is more to the story. Some people who wind up addicted did come from very dysfunctional homes, and some even had parents who were supplying the drugs.

The majority of moms and dads I come into contact with are good parents. They did their best, but despite everything right they did, things went very wrong. Now, on top of their broken heart, the inevitable guilt and the shame, they are burdened by society's stigma.

Unless one has lived on the Roller Coaster From Hell, watching helplessly as your son or daughter self-destructs, it is wise not to point fingers. Until you have spent years grieving your child, while they are still alive, it is best not to judge. We shouldn't jump to conclusions until we have traveled a particular road. It takes courage to understand and to be empathetic.

We are in a time where awareness is greater for all sorts of diseases, conditions, and situations. With the ubiquitous nature of social media, there has never been a time when there are more platforms for people to speak out. I see the coating of shame falling off of women and men every day. Society as a whole is changing, but most of us cannot afford to wait in hopes that over time society will change. We need to be the change.

I am far from shy and can engage in conversation with anyone, and I love to tell stories, laugh and meet new people. However, I spent five decades protecting my emotions. I was not one to air out my dirty laundry in public. I am not particularly fond of gossip, and I like to mind my own business most of the time.

When I realized it was time to take a stand, though, I took it. Society can think whatever they want about me because I know the truth. I am standing for the truth.

Hiding your story is just another form of control – trying to control what others think or feel about you. People are going to think whatever they want to think, so you should stop trying to manage their thoughts and feelings by covering up the truth of your story.

Whatever stigma you have been living with – stand for your truth. If someone wants to judge you, let those people cast the first stone. Nobody lives without sin. Stop allowing what others think or what you might "think" they are thinking to dictate your happiness and self-worth.

Perfectly Imperfect

A friend told me she is disappointed after every holiday. The events never play out in the way she envisioned. As she explained how she felt after a recent holiday, I recalled how after many holidays I had felt the same. Our control freak tendencies create scenes in our minds of nearly every moment of the event, right down to conversations. My friend wanted everything to be perfect. I wanted a Christmas that played out like a Hallmark movie. We both created unrealistic expectations.

The problem is Hallmark movies are not reality, and the people who are joining us at our holiday events are not perfect. When we play out the details of a gathering, it is never going to go as planned; after all, our guests don't receive a script.

I had long since stopped having expectations of holidays, considering Jamie had only been with us for a handful of them in the last half of her life.

However, I tried to make other events "perfect." Four months after Christmas was our family reunion and golf tournament. It was also the weekend we would sprinkle Jamie's ashes and have our private family memorial.

It was our nineteenth annual golf tournament and family reunion weekend. The first ten or so years it was only a small tournament with my parents and my generation. The next generation joined us a few years back, and it has turned into an incredible few days; one that everyone looks forward to each year.

Since Jamie's cousins started attending, it became incredibly difficult for me. As much as I loved having them with us, seeing my siblings enjoying the company of their adult children and watching the cousins having fun together, hurt my heart. Jamie loved her family very much, and I knew how she loved these times together, so it was hard not to miss her more than ever during these long weekends.

Much of the festivities are at our house, and it is a lot of work to host, especially the big party after the golf tournament. My nature is to want everything to be perfect, so everybody has an amazing time. I don't want anyone to travel to town and then have to work, so I take much of the burden on myself. I did it for years, and each time was left feeling as if the days flew by and I had missed most of the fun.

This past year, I decided to stop trying to make everything perfect. Rather than make all of the food, we had some people come and set up a taco bar, serving tacos and trimmings until everyone had enough to eat. Someone else made blended drinks and served them poolside. Everyone, including me, had an amazing time. For me, it was the best golf tournament/family reunion in its nineteen-year history, which doesn't make the most sense considering the timing of this one and the hole I now had in my heart. It was due to my conscious effort to stop my need to control or to strive for perfection. It was my realization that every moment is precious. Time seemed to slow down a bit, and I was peaceful and present.

Jamie's memorial was the last day of the long weekend, so that should have been hanging over my head and my heart during the festivities, but it wasn't. On Sunday, we had a simple brunch, watched a touching video, placed her ashes under a palm tree, and let a beautiful box of butterflies fly free. The day was loosely spontaneous, and it turned out "perfect."

After the service, some family members left for the airport, and others back to where they were staying, to pack up and head out. A handful of us floated in the pool, reminiscing about the fun we had.

A few days later, Sean and I were talking about the weekend, and he said,

"You know what was cool, mom? You didn't make the weekend all about Jamie. Each event was about that specific event. Then on Sunday morning, it was all about Jamie. But then when the Memorial was over, it wasn't about that anymore either."

Not attempting to make everything exactly as you think it should be, or to play out every scene in advance will allow you to live more in the present and to enjoy the event in a whole new way.

I like order. Benjamin Franklin said, "A place for everything, and everything in its place." Benjamin and I would have gotten on famously with regard to organization. Rich is a neat and tidy guy but in his own sort of way. If something needs to be put away, he often sticks it in the first available place rather than where it goes, or at least not in the spot I had designated. To my logical brain, this makes perfect sense that things go back where they belong. I don't want to spend any time looking for something and wouldn't have to if it were put back in its place. This has been a small issue for us for the past twenty years. When I cannot find something, I stand there and picture where Rich might have placed the object. I try to envision where he was and what he was doing the last time he used the item, and then I start looking around at where he might have tucked it away.

I know I shouldn't let this bother me, but truthfully, it drives me a little bit nuts. Ben would get it.

Life is messy; people are not perfect. One key to happiness is to stop trying to make everything perfect. Go with the flow more, and you just might find parties, holidays, get-togethers, and even daily life will turn out perfectly imperfect.

I am working on it.

<u>Choose Happiness</u>

I had this false notion after Jamie's death that the Beast would leave me alone; find someone his own size to pick on. Like a lot of sore winners, though, he didn't stop kicking me while I was down.

We have stepped back into the ring many times in the last year or so. The difference is that the rounds are much shorter now. For the most part, I have the upper hand. However, there are days when he sucker punches me, and I stagger around for a bit before I find my footing.

Sometimes he lands a strategic jab right at the hole in my heart, but I have learned to embrace the hole and can roll with the punches. The last time this happened was just last week, and I was hit pretty hard. It was a one-two punch, aimed at my self-worth. I will admit it rocked me for a couple of days and the Beast was no doubt smiling. Unfortunately for him, he got a little cocky and let his guard down. When I was finished allowing my emotions to run their course, I stood up taller and stronger than I was when he landed the punches. The Beast is a bully for sure, but he has met his match.

Every now and again, the Beast offers me another spin on the Roller Coaster From Hell. He makes a pretty good case for stepping on board. This time, he argues, it would be a ride of justice for Jamie.

If there were ever a time for me to don my Supermom Cape again, it would be now. I could get on the Roller Coaster of Justice, and ride it until somebody was behind bars; until there was justice for my daughter.

I have stepped onto the ride a few times. Every now and then I watch a 48 Hours or Dateline NBC episode about a senseless murder. In many of these cases, it was the family's diligence that kept the case alive. I have come to expect after such episodes that I will have certain feelings. I start to think maybe I should get down to the police station and start hounding the detectives.

I am sure my Beast has a twinkle in his eye, knowing I have a hard time resisting the Roller Coaster of Justice. He wants me to put my energy anywhere but helping other women to stand. Sadly for him, after a few twists and turns, the roller coaster starts to feel pretty familiar to me. The circumstances are very different now, but I know where this ride is headed. We are going to stop at all of the familiar places - helplessness, hopelessness, frustration, anger, self-pity, guilt, and depression. The ride will take me far from the happiness I have worked so hard to reclaim.

In every moment of every day, we have choices. Choose happiness.

LIVE
COURAGEOUSLY

"Have I not commanded you? Be strong and courageous. Do not be afraid; do not be discouraged, for the Lord your God will be with you wherever you go."

Joshua 1:9

Of Course, It's Easier Said Than Done

I talk a great deal about courage. Constantly, I remind people they need to stand up and take down their Beast. In reply to those urgings, I sometimes hear,

"It's easier said than done."

Well, of course, it is. Everything is easier said than done. Saying something takes moments. Making real change takes time, often lots of time, effort, and even some financial resources. It takes action, and it takes courage.

Using the fact that it is easier said than done as an excuse is just that – an excuse.

If you have ever played a sport, I highly doubt you stepped onto the field or court and immediately were the star of the game. Anyone who has mastered a musical instrument knows full well the hours of grueling practice. Learning any new skill requires serious work and comes with failures, frustrations and moments of feeling like giving up.

If you have been using the excuse that making changes in your life is easier said than done, I have now taken that excuse off the table. It is a given. It is not a reason to avoid stepping up and taking control of your happiness.

Everything in life worth having will take effort. Changing your life to one where you choose happiness, peace and purpose is going to be work. I will never say it is going to be easy, but the option is to live in misery; to forfeit your happiness.

Living courageously starts with a single step. Courage is built one day at a time, one decision at a time, and one action at a time. And it will take time. **This is a marathon, not a sprint.**

Attitude of Gratitude

When we are grateful for everything in our lives, it puts us into a completely different mindset than when we are in the habit of complaining. Living in gratitude is a powerful way of living. When we speak gratitude over our lives, especially when things are not going so well, it gets God's attention.

On New Year's Day, 2016, I started a 30 Day Gratitude Challenge that I shared on my Facebook page. The challenge was to write one thing you were grateful for and put it into a gratitude jar, or a journal.

I wrote at least one thing for which I was grateful on a small sticky note, folded it over and popped it into my gratitude jar. When thirty days had passed, I kept going. I am getting close now to needing a third jar, having outgrown the first two.

I started my Gratitude Jar just over four months after Jamie's murder. It is important for you to get into a gratitude mode right in the middle of your storm. While it would be a big stretch for me to say I am thankful for the events of last half of her life, I am thankful Jamie is at peace. I am grateful for all I have become in the middle of the madness, and for the incredible people who have entered my life as a result of this journey.

Be on the lookout constantly for people, situations, and things that can put you in the gratitude mindset. Allow gratitude to flood your mind, flow from your lips, and onto paper. Let God know how grateful you are, and tell others. Don't keep it to yourself.

Here's the real power-packed move – being grateful for the challenges and difficulties. Yes, you heard it right. We should be grateful, even for the Roller Coaster From Hell. This is not to say we shouldn't get off as soon as possible, but it is crucial to learn the lessons presented while on the ride and be grateful for them. Everything we go through is an opportunity to grow and change; to see things from a different perspective. These huge, scary life events provide the most opportunity to build courage.

Having a positive and empowering attitude is what I call your Battle Changer. Add gratitude to your attitude, and it will change your life.

"I hope you never lose your sense of wonder.
You get your fill to eat but always keep that hunger.
May you never take one single breath for granted."

~ "I Hope You Dance" Lee Ann Womack

Crossing the Courage Line

"You have plenty of courage, I am sure," answered Oz.
"All you need is confidence in yourself. There is no
living thing that is not afraid when it faces danger. The
true courage is in facing danger when you are afraid,
and that kind of courage you have in plenty."
~ L. Frank Barnum, The Wonderful Wizard of Oz

I believe with all of my heart that everyone is more courageous than they think. I have witnessed far too many people standing up while the storm is raging, to think otherwise. I lived in a state of terror for years, and yet today I stand as a woman of courage. I have no doubt that every person possesses the ability to do the same.

What does it mean to be courageous? Children who are battling cancer with a smile on their little faces – this is courage. The firefighters, police officers, first responders, and soldiers who run into danger, while most people are running from danger, is tremendous courage. It takes courage to remove the shame that has covered someone for most of their life. Remaining in peace while the storm is raging takes courage. Courage is deciding to be happy while your son or daughter is living with an addiction Beast. It is about forgiving someone who you don't think deserves to be forgiven. Courage tells the truth. Courage shows up in many ways.

I have always wanted Jamie and Sean to think of me as a brave woman. I never wanted my fears to transfer to them, and I believe I was doing a pretty good job until I met my Beast, and even did a decent job of covering it up for the first few years I lived with him.

Until I had my heart shattered into a million pieces and embarked upon my journey to put the pieces back together, I really didn't understand what true courage was. Until I faced the pain of losing my child at the hands of a cold-blooded murderer and chose to forgive him, I was not confident in how courageous I could become. You find out how courageous you are when you are faced with tremendous fear and choose to look them in the eye.

I told a story in my book, "Still Standing After All the Tears" which represents many years of my life. It is a story of me being down on the mat with my Beast on top of me. Each time I would try to get up, he would whisper in my ear, or scream in my face. He convinced me I was a bad mom who didn't deserve to be happy. He told me I was selfish to stand up when my daughter was in self-destruct mode. This was just for starters. I wanted desperately to stand up and be courageous, but I had no idea how. I had never faced anything requiring this level of courage.

Taking my life back while Jamie was sticking needles in her body was excruciatingly painful. Continuing to stand up and stand strong while not knowing where she was or what she was doing, was tough. Not seeing her or hearing her voice for more than a year took strength. Standing up again, and continuing my mission, after she was murdered, took incredible courage.

People who stand up and put their lives back together after a tragedy, heartbreak, loss, or bad decisions get my utmost respect. Not allowing oneself to live as a victim after being victimized is definitely courageous.

I am especially inspired by women and men who find the courage to stand up during the storm. Most of these people had no idea they possessed courage while they laid in the carnage of their lives. It wasn't until they took a leap of faith and stepped into courage that they found out what they are made of. Every day, I witness women of tremendous courage, standing up and reclaiming their lives. They stood up at a time when they did not feel very courageous.

With two sons who deal with an addiction Beast and a daughter with Asperger's, Dawn stood up and started a Facebook group to support other Christian moms of addicts, and co-wrote her first book. She continues to develop a plan to support and guide moms.

Annelle leads support groups for women, while her son is addicted and homeless. She has now linked arms with me to continue her commitment to helping to build up other women of courage, despite the hole in her own heart.

Julie's lived in a cult from a young age until she escaped from it when she went to college. A few years later, she was raising a young daughter by herself. Julie faced financial challenges and countless health issues. Instead of complaining, she started to volunteer with the Make a Wish Foundation, granting wishes for seriously ill children. Through it all, Julie maintained a positive attitude and a grateful heart. Today she is happily married to the love of her life.

Dianne volunteers as a Court Appointed Special Advocate (CASA) while running a business and raising her granddaughter. She stands through the pain of losing her daughter-in-law, and during her son's addiction.

Monette has lived through the death of three husbands, four adult children who are either addicted to drugs or incarcerated.

She lost her daughter less than a year ago. Monette is choosing to stand up and be an example to the grandsons she is raising.

Kalen's mother died when Kalen was fourteen. She and her younger sister lived with their father who was very bitter and lost in his grief. She survived a suicide attempt and went on to earn a Bronze Star in Operation Iraqi Freedom. After her time in the military, she started a non-profit organization to support veterans. Kalen is a single mom, building a business while helping many others to build theirs.

I found some index cards in an old bible that belonged to my great-grandmother. In my eight-year-old printing, was the 23rd Psalm. I recall asking my mom to help me memorize the scripture. I am surprised I was so determined to memorize this particular one because those words terrified me. (I liked the song, "Jesus loves me, this I know" one a heck of a lot more.)

I have always been studious, so it must have been something I was asked to do in the short time I was in Sunday School. I memorized the King James Version, part of which was,

"Yea, though I walk through the valley of the shadow of death."

I had no idea at the time what this scripture was all about other than it must be a pretty scary place since it is in a valley of dark shadows and death. There were rods and staffs and oil on somebody's head. I knew there was good news because I would "dwell in the house of the Lord forever," but that was pretty heavy stuff for an eight-year-old.

Having spent years asking God to take away my pain and make my life easier, I now appreciate what King David understood when he wrote the Psalm. He didn't ask God to take him around the dark valley or to remove it altogether. He knew that in his life he would have to go through some dark valleys, but he acknowledged God had equipped him for the journey and would be with him every step of the way.

I have now walked through the darkest valley I can imagine, and God was indeed with me. Not only that, he sent earth angels to walk the journey with me.

Before I decided to get my life back, I kept waiting for something to change so I could get off the Roller Coaster From Hell. Jamie had purchased my ticket without my knowledge, and it appeared it was non-refundable and non-cancellable.

I kept hoping there would be a point in time when Jamie hit her rock bottom or a moment of clarity when she would be finished living that way. I figured at that point the Roller Coaster From Hell would come to the end of the ride, and I could get off.

The fact is the ride has no endpoint. We have to decide to get off. We have to demand that our Beast stop at the nearest platform and let us off.

I was no longer willing to live in paralyzing fear, so I didn't even care if the roller coaster was between platforms; I wanted off! I didn't wait for a stop, or for someone to yank me off the ride. I pulled the emergency brake and got off. Find the courage to get off of the ride you have been living on.

Those of us who have made the decision to live courageously seem to cross an imaginary line – the Courage Line. Once you cross it, you will never be the same again, and there is no going back.

Women like Dawn, Annelle, Julie, Dianne, Monette, and Kalen are living courageously. They have crossed the Courage Line.

"She is clothed with strength and dignity, and she laughs without fear of the future."

~Proverbs 31:25

Standing Up to Fear

The world is full of scary stuff. Terrorists are scary. Angry people with automatic weapons are scary. Standing on the edge of a cliff is scary for most people. Public speaking is scary. Telling the story you have kept hidden from the world is scary. The unknown is scary.

There are a multitude of things out there that can scare the heck out of us, especially if we spend a great deal of time thinking about how scary they are. The bottom line is that bad, scary stuff can and does happen to people, no matter what they believe.

We cannot live in complete faith while living in fear. Having said that, fear is a natural response to many things. We all feel fearful at times, even courageous people. Fear is unavoidable, but we must learn to stand up to our fears. We don't have to become paralyzed by them. Many of us are trying to live by faith, and not fear, but it is a big fat challenge.

The part of faith that confused me for the longest time was the disconnection between the amount of faith I built and how easy my life should become. It seemed there should be some direct correlation between faith and how things work out for us. I know for a fact that everything does not work out okay and that God is not a good luck charm, but still. It seems only fair that the amount of faith one has should at least give us some sort of a break from hardship and pain. It should provide a pass from at least some of the fears we have to face.

The deal should go something like this - I would put my toe in the faith waters, and then God would tell the Beast to ease up a little bit. I would gain a bit more faith, then God would reward me by telling the Beast back off even more. This would result in a ton of faith, and before long the Beast would be told to leave me alone altogether. This sounded like a pretty decent deal to me, considering I had to go on blind faith and God knows everything.

No matter how much faith I built, scary things did not stop happening, and in fact, things got scarier. My faith had no bearing on Jamie's life. While the scary stuff of my life did not lessen with faith, my fear of it did, over time.

For reasons we will never completely understand, God will not remove all of our scary situations. It is up to us to take our gifts, become stronger, and take a stand against those fears.

I live in a small town, and the house where Jamie most recently lived and died, is less than five miles from our home. At the same time, it is a world away. I don't typically drive in that area, but one day a few months back, freeway construction caused me to detour toward her neighborhood. I had been avoiding the area like the plague, so the moment I made the right turn that would head me in that direction, I got a sick feeling in the pit of my stomach. I was tempted to turn around and go way further out of my way to another street that would take me back over the freeway and away from the scary place.

Something inside of me told me to keep driving. As I did, I began to pray. I prayed for all of the people suffering as Jamie did, for those who were in that world she had become a part of. I came to the rehab center where Jamie had been twice and kicked out of twice. Reluctantly, I turned down the street and stopped in front of the building where she stayed.

I knew it was time. This was the moment when I would drive down the street where she was killed. I would face another fear.

I didn't know the exact address, but I took out my phone and located the news report, showing the street name and block numbers. Before I punched it into my navigation system, I sat for a moment and cried. Then, I took a deep breath and let off the gas, moving slowly in the direction of the place where Jamie died.

It was a short street, only a few blocks long. The small tract houses were definitely nothing fancy, but none of them were the drug house I had conjured up in my mind. I pictured garbage and broken down cars everywhere; drug dealers on the streets. It was the middle of summer in the desert, so nobody was even outside. The houses are all modest, and some didn't have much of a yard, other than desert sand, but some of them had neat, well-kept yards. I drove slowly, wondering as I passed each house if it was where Jamie took her last breath. Then I realized it didn't matter. This is the neighborhood where she lived, and where she was loved.

I prayed as I drove up the street, shed a few more tears, and then drove away. As I did, nobody shot at me; no monsters jumped out in front of my car. There was absolutely nothing scary about the street. I faced my fear, and it brought me a strange sense of peace.

After the twists and incredible turns of my life, I have come to a place where I finally understand this faith over fear thing. With God on my side, I can face any fear I set my mind and heart to face. No matter what the future holds, God will be there with me, and he will make sure I have people to walk alongside me. I know he has equipped me for battle, and for loss, disappointment, and heartbreak. I have faith that peace is possible right smack in the middle of the storm.

Even after I developed a deeper faith in God, the missing piece to my faith puzzle was this – the faith in me. Believing in a God, I could not physically see, hear or touch, turned out to be easier than believing in myself.

God definitely gives more in this relationship and deserves most of the credit, but while you are busy giving God his due credit, give yourself some too. The fact is God gives you what you need, but when you have faith in those gifts, and use them to face your fears, and to become who you were meant to be – that is all you.

<u>Faith to Get Out of the Way</u>

While I had been pulling out every psychological tactic I knew to convince Jamie to get control of her life, mine was out of control. I was going through the motions of life, but I was fast becoming a person I didn't like very much.

"Battle your Beast."

"Stand up and fight."

"Take control of your life."

"Get the help you need."

"Do the work."

"Think about the impact your actions have on the family."

"You're breaking my heart."

"I know addiction is hard, but so is watching your daughter on a freight train, headed for a brick wall. Try that on for size!"

It was statements such as these that I said to Jamie repeatedly. It frustrated me she didn't seem to want to put forth the effort or fight very hard. I was heartbroken, mad, and confused as to why she was not giving her all to beat her Beast, or to stay that way during the few short periods when she was clean. I had a hard time understanding why my profound statements or guilt-ridden comments never caused her to stand up and fight.

139

I continued making those statements while I was simultaneously crying in my safe refuge, the closet. I was self-destructing, yet I was giving Jamie advice on how she should live a victorious life. I was telling, but not showing.

We do that. We tell people all the time what to do. We give advice – solicited, and more often, unsolicited. We are quick to tell people what they should do, but how often do we show them?

We have no business trying to control somebody else's journey. In fact, we should mind our own business. We need to get out of the way and allow them to do the work necessary to find their way. I was always there to stand with Jamie, but it was high time I began to respect the choices she was making, whether I liked them or not. I had to respect the fact that it was her life.

One definition of respect is: "deference to a right, privilege, privileged position, or someone or something considered to have certain rights or privileges; proper acceptance or courtesy; acknowledgment."

I began to acknowledge and accept that Jamie's life was hers and as painful as it was, she had the right to live her life in the way she chose. I needed to trust that God was still whispering in her ear.

Would I have made different choices for her – yes. Did I still wish the facts were not the facts, and I could save her – yes. Did I hope and pray every single day I would get the call from her saying she was ready – yes.

I have no control over the future, so I started to realize the best thing I could do for everyone, including Jamie was to get my life in order; make myself better. I had to save me, or there was not going to be a "me" standing next to Jamie if and when she finally decided to fight.

I wore my Supermom Cape for at least thirteen years. There is nothing wrong with moms supporting and helping, and sometimes coming to the rescue of their sons and daughters. It became a big problem when I had worn the cape for so long trying to save Jamie from herself and her addiction Beast, that it was strangling me. I wore it long after I knew my help was not helping Jamie, but it was destroying me. At first, I thought if I took off the cape, it meant I was giving up on Jamie, but I finally admitted I never had control over her in the first place. Taking it off would allow me to gain control over my own life, to be an example. It would mean I was getting out of Jamie's way; out of God's way.

When I removed the cape, I was strutting around as if saying, "Yep, that's right. I'm not doing that anymore. Done. Finito."

Before long I was tearing through the house trying to find the cape again. It felt as if a part of my body was missing. The false sense of control the cape offered left me feeling helpless. My feelings went back and forth between feeling I had abandoned Jamie and feel free and hopeful.

For the most part, I stayed away from the cape, and I got on with the business of making myself better, of becoming an example Jamie could look up to, rather than a hypocrite who was self-destructing while I barked out advice.

Since Jamie's death, I have been tempted to use the cape a few times. As I explained before, I wanted to use it to become the justice police. I have wanted to use it for Sean. The natural reaction to losing one child is to start trying to make sure you won't lose another, by controlling all aspects of their life. Sean is not living with an addiction Beast, but there are many other ways in which I could come to his rescue. The fact is the best thing I can do for him is to continue letting him know how much I love him and will always stand with him, but I trust him enough to make the right decisions. I believe in him even when he falls down, and that he has the courage to get back up. I let him know he has a God that is directing his steps if he chooses to follow.

If we expect people to be strong and courageous, we better be willing to become strong and courageous ourselves. By the time I stood up to fight, it was way past the time I should have been showing, rather than telling.

Whether or not you like the direction another person's life is going, you don't have the right to tell them what to do. When we think of cape-clad people, Superheroes come to mind. So, you may be tempted to think wearing a cape trying to save another person takes courage, but it is actually removing it that takes the courage. Respecting another person's journey, and allowing the future to unfold without trying to control their path is not natural, but it is courageous. Having faith in them is courage. Stepping out of the way and allowing God to be their guide takes faith, and it takes courage.

<u>The Big Picture</u>

Most of us have a fairly myopic view of the world. We constantly focus on how things affect us, rather than considering many things we experience might be part of a bigger picture.

More than once while Jamie was in rehab, she talked about becoming an addiction counselor. She felt she could identify with and help others to live free from the addiction Beast.

To say I was disappointed that she would never become a counselor, write her story, or speak with me on a stage one day, could be the understatement of the rest of my life. I was shocked and disappointed and thought God got this one wrong. Jamie's testimony could have been powerful, and I found it hard to imagine why he would not have caused Jamie to get clean. Why he would not have stopped the murder, giving her more time to find her way to her purpose – the one I had settled on.

We all have ideas about how our life should go and how the lives of our children should turn out. It is good to set goals, and I believe in visualization. It is important to have dreams. We simply have to be careful not to cling to one vision of our life story. When the direction of your life takes a drastic turn, look for meaning on the new path. Be willing to embrace what will be.

In the song, Que Sera, Sera (Whatever Will Be Will Be), first sung by Doris Day in 1956, the chorus goes:

Que sera', sera'

Whatever will be, will be

The future's not ours to see

Que sera', sera'

What will be, will be

The first part of the song is a little girl asking her mother what her future will be. The next part occurs later in her life when she asks her sweetheart what lies ahead. The last part is when she has her own children, and they begin to ask what they will be. The chorus above is the answer to each question.

The future is not ours to see. While we strive and work toward certain things, we must learn to accept "what will be, will be."

We didn't see the direction of Jamie's life coming; it was a hairpin turn. My vision for Jamie's life was vastly different from how the last half played out. My life is nothing as I had imagined.

I know God did not cause Jamie's addiction or her death, but he didn't stop it either. There are so many things he could have done to stop this evil, yet he did not.

It is written that God works for the good of those who love him and have been called according to his purpose. It was a challenge for me to understand what sort of purpose had while she lived in a world of addiction and danger. I found it difficult to grasp how allowing Jamie to be murdered could, in any way, work out for good.

Eventually, I started to think about Jamie's life in a different way. Even in her world of drugs and illegal activity, it was possible she had a purpose. I don't know what her everyday life was like while she was away from me for long periods of time, but I just bet she had a positive impact on some people. I will never know how many lives Jamie may have touched in ways I will never understand. She may have lived out her purpose right there in the middle of her chosen world.

Maybe that was just part of the story. Nobody will ever hear Jamie speak, or tell her story. They will never sit across from her as she guides them through a difficult period of their life. She will never personally help someone to stand over the top of their addiction Beast, but her story is making a difference through mine.

Perhaps both of our life paths were laid out before us, and certain events were allowed to occur in order to help change the lives of many others. Maybe it was never just about Jamie or me, but part of a bigger picture neither of us understood; one I am now seeing as just the tip of the iceberg.

It is possible that, through my work, Jamie will impact more lives than she ever would have as a counselor. Maybe, just maybe, God really does bring good out of bad.

<u>Fighting the Right Battle</u>

It was beyond exhausting. Day after day, after week, after month, after year, I fought. I prayed, yelled, screamed, negotiated, pled, convinced, got mad, tried to control, gave up, and started the whole cycle over.

Jamie was lost, and I had to save her. It was pretty obvious - I was her mother, and it was my job. Her age had nothing to do with the responsibility I felt. I have always been a person who could make things happen, but with regard to Jamie's addiction, I couldn't make anything happen. It was by far the most frustrating and helpless period of my life.

If there is not a word for "beyond exhaustion," there should be. Anyone who has lived through years of a loved one's active addiction has lived in this state. Other people who have lived through other ongoing heartbreak, illness or worry can surely identify.

Being a fighter, I didn't want to give up. I never wanted to give up on Jamie, but at the same time, I couldn't fight this losing battle anymore. I was beyond exhausted mentally, emotionally, spiritually and physically.

When I first stood up to fight for my own life, I was so exhausted, that I wasn't sure I had anything left in me. If I didn't have the energy to fight Jamie's Beast, how was I going to take on mine?

It turns out the reason I was beyond exhausted, is that I was fighting the wrong battle. When we try to change or fix other people, it is a losing proposition. It is like beating your head against the wall, swimming upstream, or running on a hamster wheel.

"Beyond exhaustion" can occur when you are trying to fight somebody else's battle – a battle you have no chance of winning. If you feel as if you are too tired to fight, or have no fight left, it is quite possible, like I was, you are fighting the wrong battle.

Standing up and reclaiming your life is hard work, and there will be times when you are tired, but there is a tremendous amount of energy created when we empower ourselves by paying attention to our own battle.

When I stood up to fight, I discovered I had a lot of fight left in me. When you stand up to fight, just make certain you are fighting the right battle, and you will discover you too have a lot of fight left in you.

<u>Courageous Choices</u>

The Beast loves fear; he counts on it. We live in an age where it has never been more critical for us to stand up and live courageously. At the same time, there has never been a time when courage appears more difficult to obtain. We live in a fear-based society. The internet, social media, and instant information we have at our fingertips means we are constantly bombarded with sad and horrific stories. The media seems infatuated with negative, shock value news. Life seems to get harder all the time.

I don't know about you, but while I have identified with miserable people at times, I have never envied a single one of them. It is the people who are happy when they have every reason not to be, who inspire me. Women, who live in peace while life's storm is raging, are those who give me hope. People who step outside of their incredibly difficult circumstances and make the world a better place make me believe I can do it too.

I know what it is like to live in paralyzing fear, just biding my time. I know the torment of standing helplessly by while my child self-destructed. I understand how hard it is to stand up and take your life back while the storm is still raging. I live with a gaping hole in my heart after the loss of my daughter. I know firsthand just how tough it is to fight off depression and sadness during tremendous grief, but I also know lying down on the mat is no longer an option.

Happiness is not a series of events that "happen" to you and allow you to be happy. It is not something we should wait for, but rather a decision we choose to make. Happiness is a state of mind we are capable of achieving, even during the most challenging of circumstances. If you are courageous enough to find happiness during the storm, you are more likely to keep it.

Peace does not come to you once your life is smooth sailing. It happens in your spirit and allows you to remain in a state of peace, even during trials. It is a gift from God, but you have to be willing to accept it, and to do your part to become peaceful and to remain at peace.

Purpose is what makes life worthwhile, even after all hell breaks loose. Living beyond yourself, and using your gifts and talents to make a difference is truly living.

I am still standing after all the tears, and in fact, I have stood during the tears. Your circumstances might be quite different than mine, from others, but no matter what, you too can learn how to stand up and to remain standing.

I don't have magical powers giving me a special ability to rise above my circumstances. Neither do others who have done the same. In fact, I am not much different from you. I am just a woman who decided to stand up and fight her life. If I can do it, then so can you.

You are tired of being miserable, or you have lived in misery and don't plan on going back there. You are ready to figure out how to be happy again. You want to live in peace, and to start living out your purpose.

Okay, maybe this is all too much for you right now. Perhaps you would settle for just being happy some of the time. This would be a great first step. However, I must warn you - if you truly begin to understand the perspectives here and to change your thinking, you might wind up being happy most of the time.

If you implement the Nine Actions to Battle Your Beast mentioned at the end of this book; you will learn how to put the pieces of your shattered life back together. You just might even find your purpose.

Life is a battle. If you want to live in peace, to be happy as much of the time as possible, and to live with purpose, you are going to have to fight for these things. No matter what situation we are going through, there is always a choice. Choose courage.

When the Beast reminds me of my loss, I choose courage. When I become frustrated that there is no justice for Jamie yet, I choose courage. When I doubt myself, I choose courage. When the purpose I am living out gets especially difficult and exhausting, I choose courage. When the Beast drops fear on my doorstep, I choose courage. When I am tempted to become unhappy again, I choose courage.

When the hole in my heart aches, I remember that I too have crossed over the Courage Line and there is no going back.

SAY "YES" TO PURPOSE

What we are is God's gift to us.

What we become is our gift to God.

~ Eleanor Powell

New Prayer

Sometimes we have to pray a new prayer. My morning prayer; the one I had requested for years was no longer a prayer that was no longer an option. I prayed for the miracle of Jamie's healing from addiction, and instead, it was answered with her death.

It's not that I wanted to keep praying for the miracle; I had accepted my reality. It was more about me feeling lost as to how to begin my morning prayers. The miracle prayer was not the only thing I prayed about so I could have just started talking with God about other things, but I was having such a hard time figuring out what to say.

When you pray the same opening prayer morning after morning for years, it throws you a little off balance when those familiar words come to mind, and you realize they no longer make sense.

One morning it came to me as if it was the most natural thing in the world. It felt like the thing I should have been praying first thing each day, all along.

"Thank you for another day and another opportunity to make a difference."

There are times in our lives when we have to accept reality, but it does not mean we have to give up on life. We may just need to dream a new dream or be open to a new path. It may be time to pray a new prayer.

Letting Go of the Leash

My mom's dog, Bailey takes herself for a walk. Not really, but it looks that way when my mom clips the leash to her collar. Immediately Bailey grabs the leash and heads for the door as if she is taking herself for a walk. Imagine if Bailey took herself outside and ran into the street only to be hit by a car. She needs the safety of my mom at the other end of the leash.

We do something similar. The safety of God's lead is attached to us, but we keep trying to take hold of the leash. Sometimes we even run out into the street.

Allowing God to lead us can be tough since it can be much easier to focus on things that are tangible; those in which we can attach an outcome to the action. Things we can see.

My capabilities have often led me to "do it myself." I am a quick thinker and learner, so it can sometimes seem easier that way. You know, go it alone; not bother God with the small stuff.

We make the mistake of thinking God is only going to guide us through the big stuff. We believe he has far too many things to be concerned about than our minor problems. The fact is that while he cares about the big stuff, God also cares about the small stuff. He cares about all of our stuff.

I started to get out of my own way and accept God cares about every aspect of my life and that we really are in this together, God and me. You and God are in it together too.

It has made my communication with God more of conversation throughout the day. Allowing him to lead me in the small areas of my life makes it much easier when it comes to the big things.

I like being a leader. It is a huge responsibility I do not take lightly, but every leader needs a leader. With my team player and life-long learner mentality, I am working very hard to let go of the leash.

While God does not force you to do anything, it is worth letting him take the lead. Consider letting go of the leash.

The Empowerful Zone

Comfort Zone

Many people live in what is considered a "Comfort Zone" when in reality, they are anything but comfortable.

Some people live in the Comfort Zone of not taking chances, or changing. Some stay in their Comfort Zone because they are too lazy to make a change. Others have become complacent; accepting this is all there is to life. Fear keeps many people from leaving the Comfort Zone and stepping into the unknown. The ego keeps us from potentially looking like a fool. It is easier to stay "comfortable" than deal with an uncomfortable period of not knowing what we are doing long enough to figure out what we are doing.

We were not meant to live in comfort or complacency. We are here to make a difference; to live out our purpose. We have all been given incredible gifts, talents, and experiences that are to be used, not wasted. The human brain is capable of so much more than the ways in which we use it. When you consider all of this, the Comfort Zone suddenly doesn't sound so comfortable.

I was terrified of public speaking, but then who isn't? In most surveys, it rates near the top of the fear list. The first time I spoke publicly was in oral communications. It was in a high school class where I knew everybody, but I was so nervous. It was probably the scariest thing I ever faced in my high school years.

The first time I spoke in public was at a small business meeting, and once again, I was terrified. At the same time, something inside of me was urging me to do this. Before I spoke, I went around the room and introduced myself to every person I could, so when I stood in front of the room, I was looking out at somewhat familiar faces.

A year or so after that, I reluctantly agreed to co-emcee an event with several hundred attendees. The audience would include some very experienced and skilled speakers.

On the morning of the event, the other emcee came down with laryngitis. I was shaking when I took the stage, but I had planned to use humor (my go-to place) when asking the crowd to be mindful of cell phones, and some other event business. It was going great, and I felt pretty comfortable after about a minute or two on stage, but then I heard someone below the stage trying to get my attention. One of the women putting on the event was whispering very loudly,

"The National Anthem!"

"Oh crap," I thought. The first thing this company always did was play The National Anthem, and I had gone right into to my humor routine. Somehow I had to eloquently get myself off the stage while the National Anthem played and then return as if nothing out of the ordinary happened.

As a professional speaker now, I can tell you that being an emcee is not as easy as it looks. You have a certain outline to follow, but the best emcees know how to play off of the speakers, and that day there were several speakers on stage.

We broke for lunch, and I wasn't feeling too bad about how I had managed so far when one of the seasoned speakers caught up with me and tapped me on the shoulder. He asked,

"How long have you been public speaking?"

I looked at my watch.

"Since about nine o'clock," I answered.

He went on to tell me I was a natural and how impressed he was, especially considering it was my first stage appearance.

Had I not stepped outside of my so-called Comfort Zone, I would never have realized a gift; one that can be used to help so many others.

The Comfort Zone is one of laziness, complacency, and fear. You need to step out of the Comfort Zone and into the next zone, in order to make it on to the Empowerful Zone, which is where the magic happens.

Uncomfortable Zone

The Uncomfortable Zone is painful, so it is nobody's favorite place. It is the space you will have to enter once you leave the Comfort Zone on your way to the Empowerful Zone.

It is the place where you take those chances as I did with public speaking. It is a place where you learn something new, look like a fool, or fall flat on your face. It is the place of growth and change.

The danger of the Uncomfortable Zone is that people can get stuck there just as easily as in the Comfort Zone. Often, when we hear about a woman who is in an abusive relationship, and she keeps going back, we automatically assume this has become her Comfort Zone. There are likely many reasons she doesn't leave this situation, including fear, but I doubt comfort is one of them. There is nothing comfortable about being abused.

I lived in the Uncomfortable Zone for those years between all hell breaking loose and my decision to stand up and fight. When I looked in the mirror, I recognized the woman staring back at me, but I barely knew the person I had become. The once confident, capable woman who was searching for her purpose was replaced with a hopeless, helpless, depressed, sad woman, simply existing. It was beyond uncomfortable, but I didn't know how to leave.

The Uncomfortable Zone, like the Comfort Zone, should be a temporary place. We should all be headed to the Empowerful Zone.

The Empowerful Zone

The Empowerful Zone is a place where you feel powerful and empowered. The word Empowerful is one I inadvertently made up a few months back when I misspoke. I was talking about being powerful, and how certain things are empowering and I said "Empowerful."

When I began to write this section, I was going to simply talk about the difference between the Comfort Zone and the Uncomfortable Zone. My initial thought was that people get stuck in the Comfort Zone, and only some make it to the Uncomfortable Zone and stay there long enough for the new place to become their Comfort Zone, but there is more to this. It is not simply a dance back and forth between being comfortable and uncomfortable that propels us to growth.

The Empowerful Zone is where you want to spend most of your time. This is the place where the things we once feared are second nature. It is the place of taking chances. It is the zone where we resist our ego's desire to keep us safe from failing. It is a place that doesn't allow for laziness.

The Comfort Zone will become a place you will only want to go for rest. The Uncomfortable Zone will not scare you anymore, but rather you will embrace it, knowing it is the place of growth.

The Empowerful Zone is where you know that you are living for something beyond yourself. It is where incredible courage is developed, and purpose is lived out.

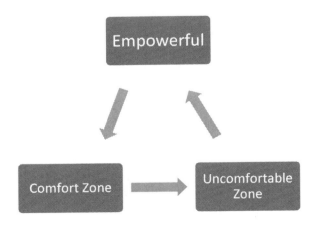

I'm So Proud of You

I no longer chased after Jamie, tried to convince or guilt trip her into recovery. I prayed, and I waited. Any opportunity I had to communicate with her, I told her I loved her as much as the day she was born. I reminded her how much I believed in her. I told her she was not her Beast, and that I would stand with her every time, she chose life. Our love for each other was never in question.

When your son or daughter is an addict, it is easy to believe they don't care about you anymore; since they seem to only think of you when they want something.

I hadn't heard from Jamie in over a year when I received an email from her. It was a loving message where she talked about her desire to be clean, to be with her family, but didn't want to be a chronic "relapser." She would let me know when she was 100% ready. I reminded her nothing in life was 100%, and when she was ready, we had some help waiting for her.

In that communication, she asked me for just one thing - a copy of my book, "Still Standing After All the Tears." She had been trying to read the random pages available on Amazon. I sent her the book, lovingly signed, and a few weeks later, I received word from Jamie that she was reading it and would get back to me soon.

Unknowingly, that email exchange would be the last we would ever have. I am so grateful for her messages that I will treasure forever. Here are some of her final words to me:

"I am seriously the most blessed girl in the world to have such an amazing mother to stand up with me."

"I still love you forever and ever, to the moon and back, and possibly twice, maybe even three times. I love you, mommy."

"I am so proud of you."

Reading these words might make you sad, which was not my intention. I want you to remember that no matter low lost somebody might be, they are watching you. I never doubted Jamie's love or admiration for me, but "I am so proud of you" is the statement that has had a profound impact on me. I believe it is a divine message for you, sent through Jamie.

This is something you should take to heart. Jamie wasn't proud of me because I was trying to save her. She wasn't proud because I was wearing my Supermom Cape, held captive by her

Beast or mine. She was not proud of me because I was crying in the walk-in closet, self-destructing with each passing day. She was proud of me because I was fighting. My happiness and sense of purpose were no longer on her shoulders. She was proud of me because I had once again found happiness. She was proud because I was making a difference in the world. Jamie was proud of my courage.

Yesterday my son, Sean sent me this text:

> "I just wanted to tell you that I am so very proud of you and I am so honored that you are my mom. God literally gifted you to me, and I couldn't be more fortunate. Jamie would be so proud of you and everything you have done. You are truly amazing."

Making the decision to stand up and fight for your life will impact those around you, in ways you cannot imagine right now. People are watching you, too. Don't let the opportunity to inspire and encourage them, pass you by.

<u>Saying YES</u>

I spent enough years trying to handle things my way. It's not that all of my years have been a struggle; they have not. There were plenty of good years in my life, and even some good times sprinkled throughout the hard years.

Life is not easy. We all go through struggles, heartbreaks, disappointment, and loss. Some people had a wonderful start to their lives, and others of us have had to meander our way through difficult childhoods. Most of us have made poor choices along the way. Certain people seem to have been dealt a much better hand in life than others, but there is no sense trying to understand why.

I have managed to do a decent job with the cards I was dealt, and the not-so-great choices I have made, but even so, I have always felt there was more to life. Even as a young girl, navigating scary waters, I felt something stirring in my spirit. For most of my life, I pushed those stirrings down and out of the way, allowing life to happen.

Life has a way of taking over and making us forget things like purpose. When my heart was shattered into a million pieces, unable to save my precious daughter, I gave up on mine, believing it was too late. I had allowed my Beast to destroy my self-confidence and self-worth.

173

The purpose I am finally living is not one I would have signed up for. It is not what I would have chosen, but as is often the case with purpose, it chose me. We can avoid it all we like, but if it is what we were put on this earth to do, it will chase us down.

The tiny bit of hope and the shred of self-confidence I found which allowed me to stand up and battle my Beast must have had something to do with purpose. At the time, I had no idea it was part of a bigger picture. I was just trying to put some of the pieces of my shattered heart back together.

The work I do is rewarding, but it is also incredibly exhausting. It takes emotional strength and endurance. Day after day, I am introduced to another family profoundly impacted by addiction, or suffering from another loss or heartbreak. This work is not for the faint of heart and takes personal discipline to keep my emotions balanced and in check.

I had a moment shortly after Jamie's death when I realized I could be free from the emotional drain, from the sad stories. I felt a brief moment of freedom.

I said to Rich,

"Now that Jamie is gone, I could just stop all of this."

He said, "Yes, you could; but you won't."

Rich understood what I was too tired to grasp at the moment - this is what I have been called to do.

We all face fears, and I guess somewhere inside of me was fear I was not worthy of a true life's purpose. It was hard to believe God would choose someone like me to go out into the world and make a difference. Why would he choose a woman who has made a lot of mistakes in her life, has done things for which she is not proud? He could, no doubt, locate someone who doesn't swear. Surely he could find someone better equipped than me for this mission. When these fears creep in, I remind myself of the disciples and what an imperfect bunch they were. If Jesus was looking for perfection, none of them would have been chosen.

Deep down, I knew I would once again stand up and remain standing. I had chosen the path of courage, and once you stand up and claim that space in the world, you won't go back. A woman of courage only goes forward. I had entered the Empowerful Zone.

When I arose from the mat for the last time, after losing Jamie, I was determined to make an even bigger difference in the world. Rather than it destroying me as the Beast had planned, something stronger rose up inside of me. I had a new resolve to allow God to take me wherever I was meant to go. My purpose was no longer chasing after me. I was all in.

I saw clearly that my entire life was preparation for a time such as this. I would stand up and fight, not only for myself but for all of the other moms out there who didn't know how to get up off of the mat. I would fight for those parents whose sons and daughters are lost in the belly of their Beasts. I would fight for the moms and dads who have lost their sons and daughters. I would set an example for anyone hurting or living with a Beast. I would shine my light as brightly as possible, even with the hole in my heart. I would show Jamie she could still be proud of her mommy.

Today, I stand on my story of hope in the midst of despair. I stand on my story of acceptance and without shame. I stand on my story of forgiveness, not guilt. I stand on my story of chaos and messiness, but no stigma. I stand on my story of loss, but not constant grief. I stand **on** my story, but NOT in it.

Remember God is not looking for perfect people; he is looking for people, who will say stand up. He is calling *you* to live out your purpose.

Will you say "yes?"

<u>Legacy</u>

For most of our lives we are going about our business, rarely thinking about our legacy; what the history book of our lives would tell. How we will be remembered by those closest to us when we are gone.

When something terrifying and heartbreaking occurs, or one lives through an ongoing heartbreak, it is easy to give up on life. The hopes we once carried disintegrate as the years pass by. There is a saying many believe to be true, "mom is only as happy as her unhappiest child." If that is true, then it is not possible for a mom to be happy while her child is lost to the addiction Beast. While I understand the sentiment, I do not agree. This suggests no mom can be happier than any of her children. While most mothers would rather their children were all happier than they are, we do have a right to be happy, even when our sons and daughters are not. I have proven it is more than possible.

For many years before Jamie died, I felt lost, alone, depressed, hopeless, helpless, unhappy, unmotivated, powerless, terrified, angry, victimized, and insignificant. Many of those same feelings returned when she was murdered. Losing my happiness would be easy, living without peace would be normal, and giving up on my purpose wouldn't be too difficult.

There may be those who feel as if my ability to stand up again, to be happy, to live in peace, and to make meaning doesn't seem right, perhaps even wrong. People may believe this proves I didn't love Jamie enough. Truthfully, I couldn't love her any more than I did, than I still do. It's just that self-destruction as a result of this tragedy, would be a tragedy in itself, and one I am not willing to live out.

Others might think my ability to forgive Jamie's killer means I don't believe in justice. Nothing could be further from the truth. I hope and pray for justice in the unsolved murder of my daughter, but as I have said before, I am not in the justice business.

The realization that Jamie's life has been taken in such a violent and senseless manner is disturbing. As the months pass with no arrests, it can be discouraging. Time keeps passing, and the case is growing colder so it can be frustrating. Rather than getting swallowed up by all of that, I choose the courageous road of peace. I stay focused on my legacy.

Mine will not be one of a sad, lonely woman whose drug-addicted daughter was murdered. My legacy will not be the grieving mother sitting at home waiting for justice for her daughter.

My legacy is to inspire people to stand up when they don't believe they have it in them. It is that of a strong and courageous woman who demonstrated to her son what it looks like to stand up and fight. My legacy is providing a roadmap and guidance for those lost in the belly of their Beasts. Mine is to empower others to get up off of the mat and find the courage to stand boldly over their Beasts. My legacy will include my vision of a line of women, as far as the eye can see, standing shoulder to shoulder with me. My legacy ensures that I am living up to the final words from Jamie,

"I am so proud of you. "

What will your legacy be? You are creating yours right now. With each passing day, you have an opportunity to not only build your legacy but to begin living it, because your legacy is being created and lived out right before your eyes.

COLLATERAL BEAUTY

Character cannot be developed in ease and quiet. Only through experience of trial and suffering, can the soul be strengthened, ambition inspired, and success achieved.

~ Helen Keller

I could write an entire book on the collateral damage of addiction, but I won't. Anyone who has walked this road knows full well the carnage left behind in the wake of the addiction Beast. There is plenty of collateral damage from all sorts of Beasts.

December 23rd, 2016, just four months after Jamie's death, Sean and two of his friends had gone with Rich and me to see "Collateral Beauty." The five of us sat in the back row of the theater, apparently all with the same sudden cold, or at least it seemed so listening to all of the sniffles.

After the movie, Sean and I walked arm in arm from the theater, still wiping the tears from our eyes.

Suddenly, I said,

"That's it, Sean! I have been trying to put words to what I am experiencing. It's collateral beauty."

Before the day at the movie theater, I had been trying to figure out how to describe the incredible blessings I had been recognizing and peace I had been feeling. While my heart ached for my daughter, and always will in some manner, I was feeling these moments of pure joy and gratitude. My purpose was becoming crystal clear.

I thought back to the people who arrived in my life while I was still living in despair, and would become such an important part of my growth, and my story. Others dropped in after I made my decision to get up off of the mat, and helped me to fight. Almost miraculously, a couple of them were placed in my path shortly before Jamie died. God carefully chose each and every earth angel I would need on my journey. While I loved and appreciated each person at the time they entered my life, I had no idea just how important each of these people would become.

During the painful years when I was down on the mat with my Beast on top of me, I spent a lot of time asking God to stop the madness that had become my life; to give me a break. While I have seen many breaks along the way, more often than not, he kept allowing me to walk through the fire. I couldn't see it then, but I am now grateful for the lessons, and for the courage it took to keep going. If not for those trials, I would not be where I am today. Continuously, I see God bringing good out of the bad. More and more, I experience the peace that surprises me.

Walking along with Sean on that crisp Arizona evening in December, I finally had a name for what I was experiencing. It is easy to see the collateral damage of a tragedy, addiction, hardship, or a life cut short, but if you look close enough, you will find the Collateral Beauty.

GOODBYE
BEAST

I alone cannot change the world,
but I can cast a stone across the
water to make many ripples.

~ Mother Teresa

Misery loves company. We have heard it a thousand times. We have watched it in action. We have been a part of it. The remarkable thing about life is that we have choices. While we have so little control over the thousands of things that surround us each day, we always have control over our happiness. We can choose peace. We get to decide whether or not we will make a difference in a world that desperately needs us. We can choose courage.

The Beast is the ultimate misery maker, thriving on causing misery and keeping people stuck in it. He convinces us we are obligated to pay God back for our mistakes by being miserable. I used to think Jamie's addiction was somehow repayment for my teenage party years, and therefore I had to endure.

Some people wear their misery like a badge of honor, but there is no honor in misery.

Even after all hell has broken loose, we have the choice to turn our back on misery. We can just walk away. We can decide who and what gets our company. Misery doesn't get any more of mine.

I spent enough precious time living in misery. Some might think I had a good reason, but I am done with it. I am over my Beast. I am officially breaking up with him.

Dear Beast,

We have spent a great deal of time together in the past, so I know this may come as a surprise, but I don't want to spend any more time with you. I guess you could say we are breaking up.

I know you enjoy my company very much and I understand how hard it is for you to let me go. For many years, I had no idea how to let you go, but now I do.

Some relationships are meant to last forever, but not ours. We had a good run. We were on the same page for many years and for most of those years, I even allowed you to run the show.

As comfortable as I became with you, we are in different places now. Before you even ask, the answer is "no." We cannot get together even on occasion. We are finished.

Don't take it too hard; there are plenty of people out there who are more than willing to spend all of their time with you. I am just not one of them.

A letter like this really should include a sentiment such as, "thanks for the memories," or "we sure had some good times together." The truth is I never had a single happy moment with you. It's not your fault though; I was a willing participant in our relationship.

Just think, with the extra time, you can focus your attention more fully on the people who are more than willing to hang out with you. They will be much better friends to you than I ever was.

So, this is it. It is goodbye. Not, goodbye for now; it is goodbye forever. Please don't call me, don't write, and don't contact me in any way. Don't think about me. Do not suggest others think of me. I will be fine without you. Misery no longer gets my company, and neither do you.

Goodbye forever,

Valerie

I have boldly taken a stand against my Beast. I am just that kind of girl. However, I doubt he is done with me. He will no doubt not take the breakup very well. It is unlikely he will ever raise the white flag and admit defeat. That is alright, though, because if by chance I find myself back in the ring, I am more than ready for the fight. A woman of courage crosses the Courage Line and doesn't look back.

This is **your** time; it's **your** moment. Take a leap of faith with me. Choose to live in victory, no matter what storm might be raging around you. Choose happiness when it doesn't seem logical. Choose peace when your life is filled with chaos. Choose to live a life of purpose when you are not sure a single person might need what you have to offer.

You don't deserve any of this because of anything you have done or have not done; neither do I. But God has offered us the free gift of mercy. So, we both deserve all of it. We deserve to live in peace and with purpose. We deserve happiness.

God says we are women of courage and we should laugh without fear of the future. He says that **you** are the daughter of a king.

The world needs **you** to live out your purpose, and it will be a much better place when you start believing this; when you stand up and start shining your light. I am standing with you.

LIFE-CHANGING ACTIONS

In a million years, I couldn't have imagined my daughter would live under the weight of an addiction Beast or that I would one day sprinkle her ashes under a palm tree. Perhaps you couldn't have imagined what has happened to you, but maybe there is something that can come out of your pain, something good, that you couldn't have imagined in a million years.

~Valerie Silveira

I wrote, "Still Standing After All the Tears" and introduced the Nine Actions to Battle Your Beast to help others who are riding their Roller Coaster From Hell.

The first time I stood up to fight was while Jamie was very lost in the belly of her addiction Beast. The Actions I took that allowed me to reclaim my life, perhaps saved my life, during my excruciatingly painful period are called **The Nine Actions to Battle Your Beast.**

I used them to put the pieces of my shattered heart back together in my darkest days and continue using them after the devastation of losing Jamie to murder.

These Actions are the reason I was able to gain control over my Codependent Enabler Beast and to keep standing as he morphed into something altogether different.

I hear from others, nearly every day, who are also putting the pieces of their shattered lives back together using these Actions. They are women and men of courage who are choosing to stand up and fight.

THE NINE ACTIONS TO BATTLE YOUR BEAST

1. **Decide to Stand Up and Fight** Decide you will stand up every time you are knocked down, and you will stay in the battle until the final round.

2. **Get On Your Spiritual Armor** The battle may be too big for you, but it is not too big for God. In a battle with a Beast, you need to call in the Big Gun.

3. **Put On Your Oxygen Mask** Give yourself permission to matter. Taking care of you, <u>IS</u> taking care of others. The best thing you can do for everyone is to become stronger and healthier.

4. **Build Your Circle of Strength** Don't step onto the battlefield alone. The Circle of Strength will change the way you look at your relationships.

5. **Change Your Attitude** This is your Battle Changer! The stories in this Action will inspire and empower you.

6. **Adjust Your Focus** What we focus on becomes magnified. Learn how your focus is affecting your life.

7. **Stop Being a Control Freak** Let go of the things you never had control of in the first place. Take off the Supermom Cape and learn the power of letting go.

8. **Stand <u>On</u> Your Story** Whatever you have done or been through - become better, not in spite of your story, but <u>because</u> of it.

9. **Make Meaning From the Madness** Your experience, wisdom, strength, and courage can make a difference in the lives of others, and you can begin right where you are. Little things are big things.

If you are not living a life of happiness, peace, and purpose, it is time to stand up and fight for your life. It is time to choose courage. Your Beast has lied to you long enough. Make TODAY the day you say enough is enough. **Fight this battle as if your life depends on it because it does.**

To learn more about The Nine Actions to Battle Your Beast, get:
"Still Standing After All the Tears," and
"Still Standing After All the Tears Workbook."

RESOURCES

Stay Connected with Valerie

www.ValerieSilveira.com

The Still Standing Sisterhood Membership

Facebook Page & Other Social Media

Podcast

Inspirational & Empowering Emails

Valerie's Other Books

Find All of Valerie's Books on Amazon

www.amazon.com/author/valeriesilveira

Still **STANDING**
AFTER ALL THE TEARS

**PUTTING BACK THE PIECES AFTER
ALL HELL BREAKS LOOSE**

NINE ACTIONS TO BATTLE YOUR BEAST

Valerie Silveira

Still **STANDING**
AFTER ALL THE TEARS

Nine Actions to Battle Your Beast

WORKBOOK

Valerie Silveira

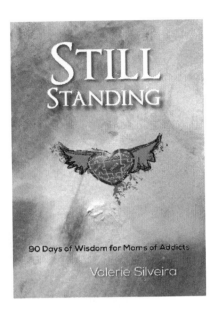

Still Standing
90 Days of Wisdom for Moms of Addicts
Valerie Silveira

Still Standing After All The Tears
Faith in the Battle Edition
Workbook
Valerie Silveira and Dawn Ward